THE
WEALTH
MANAGEMENT
EXPERIENCE

THE
WEALTH
MANAGEMENT
EXPERIENCE

THE PEACE OF MIND THAT COMES WHEN YOUR FINANCIAL ROOTS ARE STRONG

JIM HATTON

ARCHWAY
PUBLISHING

Archway Publishing books may be ordered through booksellers or by contacting:

Archway Publishing
1663 Liberty Drive
Bloomington, IN 47403
www.archwaypublishing.com
1 (888) 242-5904

Because of the dynamic nature of the Internet, any web addresses or links contained in this book may have changed since publication and may no longer be valid. The views expressed in this work are solely those of the author and do not necessarily reflect the views of the publisher, and the publisher hereby disclaims any responsibility for them.

Any people depicted in stock imagery provided by Thinkstock are models, and such images are being used for illustrative purposes only.
Certain stock imagery © Thinkstock.

For information, please write: Permissions Department, Hatton Consulting, Inc., 5090 North 40th Street, Suite 160, Phoenix, AZ 85018-2116, USA.
This publication contains the author's opinions and is designed to provide accurate and authoritative information. It is sold with the understanding that the author, publisher, and Hatton Consulting, Inc., are not engaged in rendering legal, accounting, investment-planning, or other professional advice. The reader should seek the services of a qualified professional for such advice; the author, publisher, and Hatton Consulting, Inc., cannot be held responsible for any loss incurred as a result of specific investments or planning decisions made by the reader.

Past performance may not be indicative of future results. Different types of investments involve varying degrees of risk, and there can be no assurance that the future performance of any specific investment, investment strategy, legal or tax advice, and/or product made reference to directly or indirectly in this book will be profitable, equal any corresponding indicated historical performance level(s), or be suitable for the reader's portfolio. Due to various factors, including changing market conditions, the content herein may not be reflective of current opinions or positions. Moreover, the reader should not assume that any discussion or information contained in this book serves as the receipt of, or as a substitute for, personalized investment advice from Hatton Consulting, Inc. To the extent that the reader has any questions regarding the applicability of any specific issue discussed in the book to his/her individual situation, he/she is encouraged to consult with the professional advisor(s) of his/her choosing. A copy of Hatton Consulting's current written disclosure statement discussing our advisory services and fees is available upon request.

ISBN: 978-1-4808-2363-1 (sc)
ISBN: 978-1-4808-2364-8 (hc)
ISBN: 978-1-4808-2365-5 (e)

Library of Congress Control Number: 2015919343

Print information available on the last page.

Archway Publishing rev. date: 2/1/2016

To my parents,
Dr. Richard L. Hatton and Elaine M. Hatton

CONTENTS

PREFACE

I am passionate about helping people achieve financial comfort, security, and peace of mind, and about managing their wealth so that
they can lead lives full of meaning and purpose. All of us owe it to
ourselves and the people we care about to use the tools that give us the
best chance of reaching our most important financial goals. I feel that
it is my duty to share these tools. That's what this book aims to do.

My mission to help others as a financial advisor has been driven by
the values that were instilled in me as the youngest of eight children.
I had plenty of people around me to teach me about respect, honesty,
hard work, and love—and they deserve my utmost thanks.

My father was a general practitioner in our town, and he han-
dled everything, from office visits for the common cold to labor and
deliveries in the middle of the night. When necessary, he would refer
patients to specialists (such as radiologists and oncologists) and consult with those experts to help patients with their advanced challenges.
Working together, they would create, monitor, and update plans for
patient care. The respect and dedication he showed to his patients
was inspiring.

On the day he retired, at age seventy-four, instead of throwing
himself a big party, he invited patients to come meet the doctor
who would be taking over for him. That day—a cold winter day in
Okemos, Michigan—the line of patients waiting to shake my father's
hand and thank him stretched around the office building for hours.

I remember seeing him talk with a woman who had come with her daughter and granddaughter—both of whom my dad had delivered. Three generations of a family were there to say thanks.

My father also was honest and forthcoming, to a fault. Once when he was trying to sell his car, he made a point to tell the prospective buyer about all the car's problems and things he had fixed over the years. The details that most sellers would try to hide were the details my dad made sure to share, without being asked. Why? Because he felt it was important to act with integrity, honesty, and complete transparency in his dealings. I saw him act on those values, and it left a lasting impression on how I wanted to live my own life.

There were many mouths to feed in our house. My parents had to make smart choices about money throughout their lives together. The first of my siblings began arriving in the 1950s—my mother had four children in just thirty-eight months, while she taught high school and my dad attended medical school. As more of my siblings arrived, she became a stay-at-home mom. That meant she served as the chief executive officer, chief operating officer, and chief financial officer of the house. As CFO, my mom was a master at budgeting and at juggling cash flow to satisfy all the family liabilities. From her, I learned the importance of planning, living below your means, and being conservative with your money.

I also saw first-hand the value of dedicated effort from watching my siblings. My parents scrimped and saved to pay for our educations—and, as a result, all of us attended college. However, we all knew that on the day we graduated, we'd be on our own financially. That knowledge motivated us to study diligently, get jobs lined up, and make it on our own. Seeing my brothers and sisters navigate all that inspired me and gave me the confidence that I could achieve great things if I worked hard and made smart choices.

My path to becoming a financial advisor taught me crucial lessons that I carry with me today. After college, I worked for seven years at a large medical technology company, rising through the ranks to become a manager. The firm's culture was wonderful—they cared deeply about helping customers and treating employees well. Later, I went to work for another medical company (one that turned out to be significantly less employee friendly) that merged with a competitor. As part of that merger, I saw employees in the prime of their careers laid off after being with the company for decades.

In talking with many of these employees, I learned that some had made prudent decisions about their money during their careers. As a result, they were confident about their prospects and knew they would land on their feet. Others, however, were ill prepared financially when their careers were cut short. I vowed to never end up in the situation that so many of those workers were in: middle aged and left wondering where —or in some cases *if*—they might work next. So for the next few years, I worked harder than ever and travelled constantly for the business, until I burned out.

Right about that time, my brother, Tim, called me to discuss working together as business partners. After years at a large Wall Street financial firm, he was disillusioned by the ways in which the financial services industry put its own needs above the needs of its clients. He had recently started Hatton Consulting, and we joined forces with a shared vision: to build a firm that clients could trust to deliver honest, objective investment advice and wealth management services.

It was an opportunity to take some of the most important values in my life—integrity, honesty, financial prudence, and hard work— and, as my mom and dad had done, draw on those values to help generations of families achieve their dreams. Professionally, it's immensely gratifying to work so closely with families and help them get on the right path to financial comfort, peace of mind, and security. Many of our clients have retired well and are realizing everything that is most important to them. Personally, it is hugely rewarding to be in business for myself and guide my own destiny after many years of working for other people. Together, with my brother and colleagues at Hatton Consulting, we have shaped the culture of our firm to adhere to a commitment to putting the needs of our clients above everything else.

That commitment is foremost in everything I do as a financial advisor. Like my dad, I work closely with clients to address a wide range of issues related to their financial health. When necessary, I consult with a team of specialized experts in areas like taxation, law, and insurance to coordinate clients' entire financial lives and help solve their most pressing challenges. And, remembering my dad and that car he sold, if the smartest move a client can make involves investing money independent of our firm, I say so—upfront and without being asked. Whatever is best for the client is what I will recommend at each and every step.

That lesson has been my parents' ultimate gift to me: Do the right thing, always, and over time, everything will work out well. It's an idea that I urge you to consider as you read this book and as you take charge of your financial life now, and in the decades to come.

INTRODUCTION

Wealth Management: A Superior Approach to Managing Your Financial Life

If you are like most investors today, you have a long and seemingly ever-growing list of questions and concerns about your finances. As someone with substantial assets, you have decisions to make—from how to invest your wealth so you can afford your ideal retirement lifestyle, to how to minimize taxes, to how to ensure that your heirs and other important people in your life will be well taken care of. You might be seeking to protect your wealth from being taken from you unjustly. And there's the increasingly important goal of leaving a legacy by supporting causes and charities that are meaningful to you.

Make no mistake: You have a tremendous responsibility to make wise choices about your wealth. And I know all too well that the many tasks involved in successfully managing wealth often leave investors feeling uncertain about their decisions. There's a nagging feeling that you could be making better ones, but you don't know quite how to go about it. Some investors feel almost paralyzed when they first come to our firm—unable to make *any* decisions about their money for fear of making a bad one that will put their financial future in jeopardy.

There is good news: A process exists that enables you to organize your entire financial life so that you know exactly *what* needs to be done, *why* it needs to be done, and *how* to make it happen. It is a process that replaces confusion with clarity and gets you moving in the right direction. It is a process that empowers you with the confidence that all the "moving parts" of your finances are working in concert to carry you ever closer to the goals that are most important to you and your family.

This process is called wealth management, and it's what this book is all about.

WEALTH MANAGEMENT DEFINED

You've probably heard the term "wealth management" before. Frankly, it's become ubiquitous, as more and more advisors use the term to describe what they do. But as you will see, saying you do wealth management can be very different from actually doing it.

Let's look at what, exactly, constitutes the best practices of wealth management, rightly understood. Like many people, you might think it's chiefly about the performance of your investments and how well you're doing compared to the market or your peers. But while investing is certainly a component, it is only one facet of a much broader process.

At Hatton Consulting, wealth management means something specific: It is a well-defined process designed to solve a full range of challenges for affluent investors on an ongoing, long-term basis and coordinate all of the aspects of their wealth that they must arrange in order to build meaningful lives.

There are three main components, as we practice it:

1. Investment consulting aims to position your assets around your goals, return objectives, time horizons, and risk tolerance. This is the foundation upon which a comprehensive wealth management solution is created. Investment consulting refers to portfolio design, then the implementation and monitoring of investment assets, which can generate superior results.

2. Advanced planning means going beyond investments to address your financial needs in five additional areas: tax planning, estate planning, insurance planning, asset protection, and charitable giving. *Advanced* planning involves going the extra mile, harmonizing all investment consulting decisions with your other areas of concern—ensuring that all aspects of your financial life work together seamlessly. It's a sophisticated approach that ends up simplifying your life.

3. Relationship management involves understanding your needs and meeting them over time through a consultative process, assembling and managing a network of financial experts, and working well with any professional advisors you engage (such as attorneys and accountants).

As you read on, you can think about wealth management using the following shorthand:

Wealth management = investment consulting + advanced planning + relationship management

THE BENEFITS

The majority of investors today, even those who have professional financial advisors, do not take a wealth management–based approach.

In fact, one study by CEG Worldwide found that a mere 6.6 percent of financial advisors practice the kind of wealth management we are talking about—even though many more advisors call themselves wealth managers.

For most of these professionals, the focus is on investments—allocating capital to asset classes and picking stocks, funds, exchange-traded funds (ETFs), and other investment products. That outlook, by itself, fails to take into account other factors that are huge drivers in investors' ultimate ability to achieve their goals—including their exposure to income taxes and estate taxes, as well as their ability to protect the wealth they have built over time. By stopping short of connecting *all* aspects of your financial life in a holistic way, you needlessly put at risk your future and the futures of those you care about most.

Based on my experience bringing full-fledged wealth management to my clients, I have seen four key advantages coming out of this comprehensive process:

1. Coordination. All aspects of your financial life work in concert. This mitigates the risk of having one decision negatively impact another part of your finances. It also enables you to take advantages of opportunities that can only be identified using a holistic approach. For example, combining income tax analysis with investment management can reduce other taxes beyond the ones on your investments.

2. Clarity. Wealth management, done thoroughly and well, gets you and your family organized so you can see exactly what you've got, how these different pieces are (or are not, in some cases) fitting together, and how they could be made to work harder on your behalf. The result: a sharper picture. You can make smarter, more confident decisions about your wealth.

3. Policies for dealing with life events, both expected and unexpected. Wealth management can spell out what will occur with your finances if you become incapacitated or otherwise unable to make decisions—giving you the comfort of knowing that your family will not be forced to face avoidable dilemmas during trying times and that their well-being is assured.

4. Peace of mind. Wealth management brings you a level of calm about your future that you may never have experienced before. The serenity that comes from knowing you have a process in place that is working to improve your situation at all times means that you can enjoy a largely worry-free life in retirement, focused on the things you want to accomplish.

THE CONSULTATIVE PROCESS

Investors who adopt a systematic wealth management approach use what we call the consultative process to identify challenges and implement a range of ideal solutions. At my firm, the process begins with four structured meetings with our clients, with follow-up meetings after that:

1. The Discovery Meeting. At our initial session, we conduct a discovery interview. We examine your current situation, identify the goals you would like to achieve, and decide how we can maximize the possibility of achieving them.

2. The Investment Plan Meeting. At this meeting, we present our diagnostic review of your situation and our recommendations for how we can bridge the gaps in order for you to reach your goals. This plan forms the foundation for all of our work together.

3. The Mutual Commitment Meeting. At this stage, we are ready to make a mutual decision about whether our firm can add substantial value, and whether we should proceed. Should we choose to go forward, we commit to each other to work toward achieving everything that is important to you and your family. We also execute the documents necessary to put your investment plan into motion.

4. First Follow-Up Meeting: Development of Your Wealth Management Plan. When you have multiple investment accounts, it's easy to become overwhelmed by the many documents coming to you. At this meeting, we help you organize and understand all the paperwork and reports you will be receiving. We answer any questions you may have so that you understand exactly what is happening with your money. At this point, we also begin to develop your wealth management plan. We focus on five aspects of your financial life:

- **Income tax planning** aims to produce the best possible investment returns consistent with your level of risk tolerance and to minimize the tax impact on those returns.
- **Estate planning** finds the most tax-efficient way to pass assets to succeeding generations, and to do so in a way that meets your wishes.
- **Insurance planning** assesses risks you may face related to disability, long-term health issues, and death, and then formulates responses that address those risks through the use of insurance.
- **Asset protection** is directed at protecting your wealth against potential creditors, litigants, children's spouses, and potential ex-spouses.
- **Charitable giving** helps fulfill your charitable goals. It is most effective, and tax-efficient, when coordinated with the four services above.

After that, we schedule regular progress meetings at intervals convenient to you. In those sessions, we review any major changes in your personal or financial situation since our last meeting. We recommend getting together at least annually and whenever major changes occur. If these changes mean that we need to make adjustments to your investment plan, we do so.

On a quarterly basis, through portfolio monitoring and reporting, we also review your progress. These meetings are another opportunity to implement advanced solutions that may be appropriate for your situation. We will update the plan that we developed for you, prioritize the areas of greatest importance to you, and begin to address them systematically.

Because this consultative process is something you will experience if you choose to work with our firm, we will explore each of these meetings and the steps within them in the next several chapters.

ARE YOU USING WEALTH MANAGEMENT?

The benefits of wealth management are powerful, but as you've seen, it's not nearly as common an approach as you might expect (or hope). To see whether the methods you or your advisor are currently using can meaningfully be called wealth management, review the accompanying Wealth Management Checklist. You may discover that a well-conceived wealth management process is already being brought to bear on your financial life. If so, congratulations—you are well positioned for the future and can feel confident about the path you are on.

THE WEALTH MANAGEMENT CHECKLIST

WEALTH MANAGEMENT CHECKLIST	The Wealth Management Process	Your Current Process
Has your background data (including financial, tax, estate, insurance, asset protection, and philanthropic goals) been collected and documented?	YES	
Do you have an agreed-upon process detailing how you will work with and coordinate financial decisions among all your professional advisors?	YES	
Has an Asset/Liability Statement been created? Is it being kept current?	YES	
Have your income sources and expenses been documented?	YES	
Has asset allocation been determined and aligned with your risk tolerance?	YES	
Have one-year range of returns for your portfolio been calculated and documented?	YES	
Is there a document detailing your mix of cash, bonds, and stocks?	YES	
Has a five-year cash flow been estimated, documented, and reviewed?	YES	
Has an expected, modeled investment return to meet goals been calculated and documented?	YES	
Do you have a documented process for when and how your portfolio will be rebalanced?	YES	
Do you have a due-diligence checklist for selecting and monitoring of investment vehicles?	YES	
Has a contact list of all your professional advisors (financial, estate, tax, insurance, trustee, others) been put together?	YES	
Has a process been developed to monitor investment management fees?	YES	
Are you receiving quarterly performance reports that show rates of return for your portfolio after investment fees?	YES	
Is the after-fee portfolio performance compared quarterly to the appropriate benchmark?	YES	
Is the current asset allocation compared quarterly to the target allocation?	YES	
Are current investments evaluated quarterly to see if there is any need for replacement?	YES	
Does your advisor consult with your other professional advisors to ensure a coordinated strategy is being executed properly on your behalf?	YES	

Source: Hatton Consulting, Inc.

If not, I invite you to read on to discover how wealth management will maximize your ability to achieve not just a comfortable retirement, but all that is most important to you and the people you care about most.

PART ONE

The Wealth Management Process

CHAPTER 1

The Discovery Process: The First Step to a Secure and Meaningful Financial Life

Imagine for a moment that you are about to take a road trip across the country to new and exciting destinations. Would you simply wake up, get out of bed, get in the car, and start driving? Of course not. You would plan your route carefully, identify items you'd need for your travels that you already own, and then go out and acquire the remaining items to help ensure that your journey will be smooth, fun, and successful. You'd probably even enjoy the planning phase. When you actually hit the road, you'd no doubt have some tools close by—a trusted road atlas, directions from Google Maps or a satellite navigation system—to help ensure you stay on the right course and end up at your desired destination.

Sounds obvious, right? And yet, as investors we too often forsake this type of crucial planning when we invest our money and make other important decisions. It's not surprising that so many investors today feel a bit lost or unsure about the progress they're making toward retirement and other key goals.

In this chapter, we look at how to dispel that uncertainty by conducting a thorough financial self-analysis we call the discovery process. By doing it before you do anything else with your finances, you will find yourself able to answer three questions that play a huge role in your ultimate financial success and sense of well-being:

- Where are you today?
- Where do you want to be in the future?
- How will you get there?

At our firm, we believe that this discovery process is so crucial to long-term financial success that we take each prospective client through it, step by step. What follows is what you could expect from a discovery process meeting with us.

WHERE YOU STAND NOW

You need to know your starting point in order to draw a map of where you want to go. That means, first of all, assembling the relevant account information and documents.

This can feel like a surprisingly daunting task—but it is an absolutely essential one. Many people discover that they are not nearly as organized as they imagined. Learning that everything they need is not immediately accessible can be a valuable lesson in itself. The process of organizing your financial information can create clarity and reduce the anxiety associated with pursuing big goals, such as transitioning into retirement. Peace of mind is the reward of creating this organized, streamlined financial situation.

To help you assemble the documents you need, consider the following list. It details the kind of information we ask prospective clients to bring to our initial discovery meeting. Not every item on this list may pertain to your situation, of course, but its comprehensiveness will help you minimize the odds of overlooking something important:

- the most recent statements from all your investment, brokerage, and banking accounts (including IRAs, 401(k)s, checking and savings accounts, trust accounts, and annuities)
- statements associated with your sources of income (including your Social Security Benefit Statement; pension benefit
statements from employer-sponsored retirement accounts;
deferred compensation benefit statements; statements of mil-
itary, annuity, and rental income; and other similar records)
- stock options statements
- Summary Plan Benefits Description booklet detailing your
employer-sponsored benefits
- federal and state tax returns for the previous two years
- purchase price and current market value of any real estate
- mortgage statements for any real estate holdings (including title, balance, interest rate, monthly payment, and payoff date)
- current life insurance policies and statements (including
names of the insured and the policy owner, death benefit,
beneficiaries, annual premium, cash values, and surrender
values)
- details on the following policies: medical insurance, long-
term care, and disability (premium, beneficiaries, and basic
policy data)
- list of debts or liabilities other than mortgage (such as credit
cards, auto loans, home equity lines of credit, business debt,
401(k) or life insurance loans)
- any wills or trust documents (including trusts where you may
be a beneficiary)
- household budget expense log (your core expenses)
- large known expenses other than your core expenses (automobile, major home repairs, etc.)
- your family tree, beginning with your parents and ending
with your grandchildren (include dates of birth and death)

- qualified domestic relations order (if you are divorced and have a financial commitment to or from your previous spouse)
- list of your professional advisors and their contact information

I readily admit that gathering some of this information might test your patience. But resist the urge to short-cut this step. You must have an accurate picture of your situation before you can begin to knowledgably plan for the future.

Take your sources of income, for example. Many of our clients lack clarity about what their income sources are and the rules governing those sources of income before and after they retire or begin drawing Social Security. As a result, they don't know what they've got now or what they can expect to receive from their various income sources in retirement. (If you are ready to start this inventory and are interested in learning more about sources of income and how they might factor into your retirement lifestyle, you'll find details in in chapter 6.)

The final part of this step is to collect the information you have gathered into a single form. (We'll show you an example of this kind of form in chapter 8.)

WHERE YOU WANT TO BE IN THE FUTURE

Many people have a somewhat vague notion of what they want in retirement. By developing a clearer retirement vision, it's possible to determine how much money will be needed to turn that vision into reality.

I find most people envision their future retirement as being pretty much the same as their working year, minus the work. But what will replace the many hours spent on the job each week, as well as the commute to and from the office?

This brings us to the next aim of the discovery process, to help you identify your deepest, most important wants and needs. You will find it difficult if not impossible to cope with the complex and sometimes conflicting challenges you face until you position your assets around the values, needs, goals, and issues that are important to you as a person. Only then will your wealth support all of the things you want to accomplish.

The discovery process helps you identify what's important to you in seven areas. Your answers to the types of questions shown below will enable you to develop a full picture of who you are and what you want from your retirement life. Once you have that picture, you can arrange your assets to support you appropriately.

1) Values. What is truly important to you about your money and your desire for success, and what are the deep-seated values underlying the decisions you make to attain them? When you think about your money, what concerns, needs, or feelings come to mind?

2) Goals. What do you want to achieve with your money over the long run, professionally and personally—from the most practical to your biggest dreams?

3) Relationships. What people in your life are important to you— including family, friends, religious affiliations, universities, charities, and even pets?

4) Assets. What do you own—from your business, to real estate, to investment accounts and retirement plans—and where and how are your assets held?

5) Advisors. Whom do you rely on for advice, and how do you feel about the professional relationships you currently have? Wealth management is designed to work in partnership with all of your trusted advisors to arrive at solutions that complement each other.

6) Process. How actively do you like to be involved in managing your financial life, and how do you prefer to work with your advisors?

7) Interests. What are your passions—hobbies, sports and leisure activities, charitable and philanthropic involvements, religious and spiritual proclivities, and children's schools and activities?

For a more extensive list of the issues we present to our clients, see the accompanying table, Discovery Process Questions.

DISCOVERY PROCESS

DISCOVERY PROCESS QUESTIONS
YOUR VALUES
Money means different things to different people. What's the chief value you assign to it?
What is particularly important to you concerning that value?
Is there anything that is more important than that value?
YOUR RELATIONSHIPS
Which family relationships (spouse, children, siblings, parents, etc.) are the most important to you?
How important are your relationships with people you work with?
How important are your relationships with people in the community?
Clients have different views as it pertains to religion. What is your religious orientation and how devout are you? Do you have a financial commitment with any church?
What pets do you have, and how important are they to you?
What schools did you go to? How important is your relationship with these schools?
What is the life expectancy of your parents, or, if they are no longer living, how long ago did they die?
YOUR GOALS
What would you list as your top accomplishments so far? What would you like them to be, moving forward?
What are your personal goals?
What are your professional goals?
What do you want to do for your children?
What do you do or want to do for other family members or close friends?
When you think about your money, what concerns, needs, or feelings come to mind?
If you didn't have to work anymore, what would you do?
YOUR ASSETS
How do you make money today? How is that likely to change in the next three years?
What are your other sources of income?
How do you save or set aside money to invest? How is that likely to change in the next three years?
What are your investment holdings? Explain your strategy for handling your investments as you do?
What benefits do you get from your employer?
What life insurance do you have?
What real property do you have (real estate, art, jewelry, antiques, collectibles, heirlooms)
How are your assets structured now?

DISCOVERY PROCESS QUESTIONS (CONTINUED)

YOUR ADVISORS

Do you have a lawyer? How do you feel about the relationship?

Do you have a life insurance agent? How do you feel about the relationship?

Do you have someone who helps you choose health insurance?

Do you have an accountant? How do you feel about the relationship?

Do you have an investment advisor? A stockbroker?
How do you feel about the relationship?

Do you have a financial planner? How do you feel about the relationship?

What were your best and your worst experiences with a professional advisor?

YOUR PROCESS

How involved do you like to be in the managing of your finances?

How many face-to-face meetings would you want over the course of a year?

Would you want a call about your personal situation when there is a sudden change in the market?

How often would you like phone updates on your situation?

Do you want contact by email? If so, what should the emails be about?

How often do you want an overall review of your financial situation and progress toward your goals? (At minimum, our firm schedules comprehensive annual reviews.)

Who else do you want involved in the management of your finances (spouse; other family members; other advisors such as accountant or attorney)?

How important to you is the confidentiality of your financial affairs?

YOUR INTERESTS

Do you follow sports? What are your favorite teams?

What are your favorite TV programs, movies, types of music?

What do you read?

Do you have health concerns or interests? What is your health program?

Are working out and fitness important to you? What is your fitness routine?

What are your hobbies?

What would an ideal weekend be?

What would an ideal vacation be?

What charitable causes do you donate to? Volunteer for?

Source: CEG Worldwide, LLC

Your answers to these questions can be used to create a Total Investor Profile that will serve as a roadmap—a guide so that every financial decision you make supports what you want most from life.

If, like most affluent investors, you currently work with one or more advisors, you are probably aware that most use some type of fact-finding process when first meeting with clients or prospects. But have you ever noticed that these questions usually focus on your assets and net worth? In contrast, only one of the seven categories that make up wealth management's Total Investor Profile concerns assets. Six of the seven are focused on helping you (and your wealth manager, if you use one) better understand who you are as a person.

TOTAL INVESTOR PROFILE

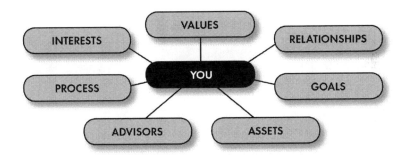

Of course, a significant part of determining where you want to be down the road depends on what that destination will look like from a dollars-and-cents perspective. No matter what your vision for retirement is, it's sure to have a price tag.

For example, you're going to want to know how much money you'll need to make work an option—not a necessity—and let you retire comfortably. Knowing numbers like that not only boosts your confidence and peace of mind, it drives technical aspects of your portfolio's asset allocation and investment selection.

To figure out the amount of annual retirement income you will need, you'll estimate your annual retirement expenses. The budgeting worksheet in chapter 7 will take you through the full range of retirement expense categories so you can make good estimates.

CLOSING THE GAP—DEVELOPING YOUR TARGET RATE OF RETURN (TRR)

The information gathered so far will help you determine the annual after-tax income need to meet your estimated retirement living expenses. The next step is to add taxes, at your net effective tax rate, to that estimate, to determine your *gross* annual income need in retirement. Often, investors' net effective tax rate falls between 15 and 25 percent.

Once you know your gross annual income need in retirement, you can add up all of your sources of income in retirement. Those sources of income may include Social Security, one or more pensions, income from real estate, money from a deferred compensation plan, and other sources. (In chapter 6, we will review the various sources of retirement income you may have.)

Then subtract the total of all income sources from your gross annual income needed. That number is your shortfall—that is, the amount of money you need to generate from your investment portfolio each year to fund your retirement.

The last step in calculating your target rate of return is to divide your shortfall by your total retirement savings. Let's assume your shortfall is $62,000 and your total retirement savings is $2,480,000. Therefore, $62,000 ÷ $2,480,000 = 2.5%. Add what you estimate inflation may be, and you will have calculated your TRR. Let's say, for example, that you expect a 3 percent annual inflation rate going forward. In that case, 2.5% + 3% = 5.5% TRR.

Here's a snapshot of how this process looks on paper:

TARGET RATE OF RETURN

EXPENSES	AMOUNT
Total Annual Expenses	$100,000
Taxes (20%)	$25,000
Gross Annual Income Need in Retirement	**$125,000**
Less: Annual Social Security Income	($20,000)
Less: Annual Pension Income	($18,000)
Less: Rental income from commercial real estate	($25,000)
Annual Income Needed from Portfolio	**$62,000**
Target Rate of Return (TRR) needed, without inflation (portfolio income needed, divided by total retirement savings)	$62,000 ÷ $2,480,000 = **2.5%**
Target Rate of Return (TRR) + Inflation (3%)	2.5% + 3% = **5.5%**

Armed with this information, you can create a portfolio with a mix of assets (such as stocks, bonds, and cash) intended to generate an annual return that matches your TRR, enables you to meet your retirement expenses, and helps you live a life that reflects not just your financial needs but also your values.

The rate of return you target, and the return you ultimately receive, will be determined in large part by the types of assets you select for your portfolio and the way in which you combine them. I'll cover those and other topics in the next chapter, which focuses on how to create an investment plan based on the information learned through the discovery process.

CHAPTER 2

Creating an Investment Plan: The Second Step to a Secure and Meaningful Financial Life

Now that you know where you stand today and where you want to be tomorrow, it's time to take steps that will enable you to close that gap. For the vast majority of investors, the first step in that process is investment consulting—the act of positioning your investment capital to reflect your goals, return objectives, and risk tolerance.

At Hatton Consulting, we follow a highly structured and disciplined process when building and maintaining investment portfolios—one carefully designed to maximize our clients' probability of reaching their goals and achieving financial peace of mind. In this chapter, we'll see why investors often underperform broad market indexes and fail to achieve their objectives. Also, I will take you through a process so you can understand what we firmly believe it takes to achieve true and meaningful investment success.

BELIEFS AND BEHAVIORS: THE KEY DRIVERS OF INVESTORS' UNDERPERFORMANCE

It's an unfortunate fact that the returns on most investors' port-folios fail to achieve their investment goals or simply meet or beat market indexes. Consider evidence from Dalbar, a leading financial services market research firm that analyzes how mutual fund investors' decisions impact their long-term rate of return. In examining the twenty-year period through December 31, 2013, Dalbar found the following:

- While the S&P 500 gained 9.22 percent annually during those 20 years, the average stock fund investor earned a return of just 5.02 percent, underperforming the index by 4.2 percent!

S&P 500 — 20-YEAR GAINS

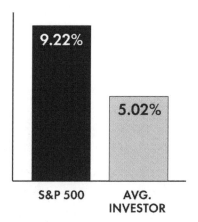

Source: DALBAR , Inc., 2014 Quantitative Analysis of Investor Behavior Study

- The Barclays Aggregate Bond Index gained 5.74 percent during that period—but the average bond fund investor earned a mere 0.71 percent. With a shortfall like that, they're not even keeping pace with long-term annual inflation at 3 percent!

BARCLAYS — 20-YEAR GAINS

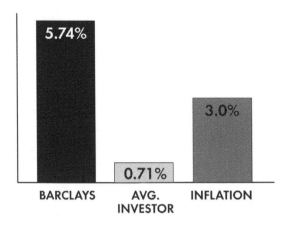

Source: DALBAR , Inc., 2014 Quantitative Analysis of Investor Behavior Study

How can so many people be getting such poor results? There are two negative drivers for the average investor: misguided investor beliefs and behavior.

First, let's explore investor beliefs. Investing can be broken down into two major beliefs:

- You either believe in the ability to make superior security selections, or you don't. Put another way, many investors believe that the key decisions they must make are which stocks they should buy or which mutual funds they need to own.
- You either believe in the ability to time markets, or you don't. That is, many investors jump in and out of the markets repeatedly in an effort to capture the good days and avoid the bad ones.

Next, consider which investors have which belief systems—and where you should be with your own beliefs. The Investment Decision Matrix in the accompanying table classifies people according to how they make investing decisions:

THE INVESTMENT DECISION MATRIX			
		MARKET TIMING	
		YES	NO
SECURITY SELECTION	YES	Noise Quadrant **1** Most individual investors Financial journalists	Conventional Wisdom Quadrant **2** Financial planners Stock brokers Most mutual funds
	NO	Tactical Allocation Quadrant **3** Pure market timers Asset allocation funds	Information Quadrant **4** Academics Many institutional investors

Source: CEG Worldwide, LLC

Quadrant 1 is the noise quadrant. It's composed of investors who believe in both market timing and superior investment selection. They think that they (or their favorite financial guru) can consistently uncover mispriced investments that will deliver market-beating returns. In addition, they believe it's possible to identify the mispricing of entire market segments and predict when they will turn up or down. The reality is that the vast majority of these methods fail to even match the market, let alone beat it.

Unfortunately, most of the public is in this quadrant because the media plays into this thinking, as they try and sell newspapers, magazines, and television ads. For the media, it's all about getting you to return to them time and time again.

Quadrant 2 is the conventional wisdom quadrant. It includes most of the financial services industry. Most investment professionals have the experience to know they can't predict broad market swings with any degree of accuracy. They know that making incorrect predictions usually means losing clients. However, they believe there are thousands of market analysts and portfolio managers with MBAs and high-tech information systems who can find undervalued securities and add value for their clients. Of course, it's the American dream to believe that if you're bright enough and work hard enough, you will be successful in a competitive environment.

As un-American as it seems, in an efficient capital market, this methodology adds no value, on average. While there are debates about the efficiency of markets, most economists believe that, fundamentally, capital markets work.

Quadrant 3 is the tactical asset allocation quadrant. Investors in this quadrant somehow believe that, even though individual securities are priced efficiently, they (and only they) can see broad mispricing in entire market sectors. They think they can add value by buying when a market is undervalued, waiting until other investors finally recognize their mistake, and selling when the market is fairly valued once again. We believe that it's inconsistent to think that individual securities are priced fairly but that the overall market, which is an aggregate of the fairly priced individual securities, is not. No prudent investors are found in the quadrant.

Quadrant 4 is the information quadrant. This is where most of the academic community resides, along with many institutional investors. Investors in this quadrant dispassionately research what works and then follow a rational course of action based on empirical evidence. Academic studies indicate that investments in the other three quadrants, on average, do no better than the market after fees, transaction costs, and taxes. Because of their lower costs, passive investments – those in quadrant four – have higher returns on average than the other types of investments.[1]

Now let's explore investor behavior and its role in producing the sub-par returns that many portfolios generate. Consider what often happens when investors get a hot stock tip from a friend or associate (summarized in the accompanying illustration.

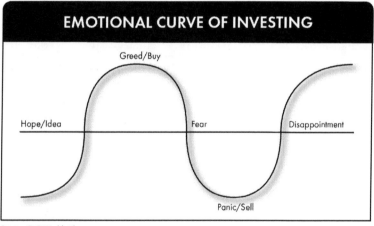

EMOTIONAL CURVE OF INVESTING

Greed/Buy

Hope/Idea   Fear   Disappointment

Panic/Sell

Source: CEG Worldwide.

If you're like most investors, you don't buy the stock right away. You've probably had the experience of losing money on an investment, so you're not going to race out and buy that stock right away, based solely on the hot tip. You're going to follow it awhile to see how it does. Let's assume, for this example, that it starts trending upward.

You follow it for a while as it rises. What's your emotion? Confidence. You hope that this might be the one investment that helps you make a lot of money. Let's say it continues its upward trend.

You start feeling a new emotion as you begin to consider that this just might be the one. What is the new emotion? It's greed. You decide to buy the stock that day.

You know what happens next. Of course, soon after you buy it, the stock starts to go down, and you feel a new combination of emotions—fear and regret. You're afraid you made a terrible mistake. You promise yourself that if the stock just goes back up to where you bought it, you will sell it and never do it again. You don't want to have to tell your spouse or partner about it. You don't care about making money anymore.

Now let's say the stock continues to go down. You find yourself with a new emotion. What is it? It's panic. You sell the stock. And what happens next? New information comes out, and the stock races to an all-time high.

These extreme emotional reactions that drive many investors' buy and sell decisions about a particular hot stock also cause investors to jump in and out of entire segments of the financial markets. This behavior can wreak havoc on your long-term rate of return if you are out of the market on the wrong days. Consider another study showing the negative impact on your investment returns of missing the very best days for the stock market over time. As seen in the accompanying illustration, Reacting Can Hurt Performance, investors who invested in a fund that tracked the S&P 500 in 1970 and consistently stayed invested for the next forty-three years would have earned a 10.4 percent annualized return on their initial investment.

But look at what happens to that return if those investors tried to time the markets. By missing just the best five days during that entire forty-three-year period, the return falls to 9.3 percent. And by missing the best twenty-five days, the return is just 6.9 percent.

REACTING CAN HURT PERFORMANCE
Performance of the S&P 500 Index, 1970-2013

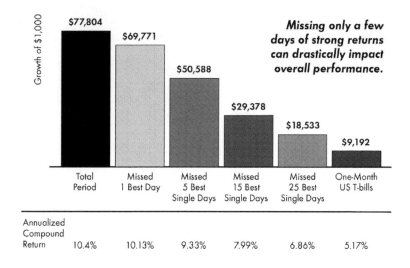

Missing only a few days of strong returns can drastically impact overall performance.

	Total Period	Missed 1 Best Day	Missed 5 Best Single Days	Missed 15 Best Single Days	Missed 25 Best Single Days	One-Month US T-bills
Growth of $1,000	$77,804	$69,771	$50,588	$29,378	$18,533	$9,192
Annualized Compound Return	10.4%	10.13%	9.33%	7.99%	6.86%	5.17%

Source: Dimensional Fund Advisors. Please remember that past performance may not be indicative of future results. Different types of investments involve varying degrees of risk, including loss of principal and there can be no assurance that the future performance of any specific investment or investment strategy will be profitable. Indices are unmanaged baskets of securities in which investors cannot directly invest. For illustrative purposes only.

We're all poorly wired for investing. Misguided investment beliefs and emotional behavior are powerful forces that cause you to buy high and sell low—exactly the opposite of what you should do. If you do that over a long period of time, you'll cause serious damage not just to your portfolio, but also to your financial dreams.

Our goal is to help investors make smart decisions about their money. To accomplish this, we help them move from the noise quadrant to the information quadrant. We create policies and procedures that remove the emotional responses and actions that can negatively impact your financial success. We believe this is where you should be to maximize the probability of achieving all your financial goals.

ALLOCATE YOUR ASSET CLASSES

Now that you understand the forces you are up against as an investor, let's focus on how to build superior portfolios.

You know from the discovery process your shortfall and the target rate of return you need to pursue with your investments. Your next step: decide how best to combine types of assets in a way that will generate that return over time with the least amount of risk necessary to get there.

Enter the concept of asset allocation. Asset allocation is a strategy where you apportion your assets among different broad categories of investments, called asset classes. An asset class is a group of securities that are highly correlated and share similar risk and return characteristics. Asset allocation has been used by investors for decades, and you're probably well aware of its basic message: Don't put all your eggs in one basket. By spreading your capital among multiple asset classes, you can generate investment gains over time while minimizing the amount of ups and downs in the value of your portfolio along the way.

THREE MAIN TYPES OF ASSET CLASSES

To do exactly that, let's start by examining the three major asset classes that you should consider for your portfolio:

1. Equities (Stocks). If you own stock of a company, you have an equity (ownership) interest in that business. Companies sell stock to raise cash for business operations and investment in growth and development. As a company performs well financially, you benefit in the form of appreciating values of your stock. Additionally, you may also receive a dividend, either in cash or as extra shares when the company declares a payment to stockholders. Conversely, if a company's financial performance is poor or if other variables negatively impact the company, the stock price may decline. Additionally, the company may decide it does not have the financial resources to pay a dividend, negatively impacting the stockholder even further. Risk and reward go hand in hand. You probably know that among the three asset classes discussed here, stocks offer the highest potential returns over the long term but also carry the most risk. Investors are compensated with higher expected returns for agreeing to accept the higher level of risk. For example, the stocks of large companies as measured by the S&P 500 index have gained 10.1 percent annually from 1926 through 2013.

Along the way to those sizable returns, however, stock investors have faced significant price swings—especially over relatively short periods such as one, five and ten years. There is no free lunch. Consider years such as 2008, when large-company stocks lost 37 percent. The upshot: Stocks tend to deliver strong returns over time, which means they belong in nearly every investor's portfolio—but they also are quite volatile over shorter periods, which means that a portfolio of stocks must be tempered by other investments.

2. Bonds. A second way that companies raise cash is by issuing bonds. Think of a bond as a loan to a company. An investor will loan cash to a company and receive a bond in return. A bond is a contractual obligation from the issuing company to pay periodic interest to the bond holder and return the principal value at some predetermined date in the future. Bonds offer attractive, but lower, potential returns than do stocks. For example, long-term government bonds, with an average maturity of twenty years, have generated annualized returns of 6 percent from 1926 through 2013 However, bond prices tend to remain more stable than stock prices—that is, because bonds are less volatile than stocks, they tend to swing less wildly over short periods. Therefore, bonds can help smooth out the annual returns of an otherwise all-stock portfolio. That said, bonds can decline in value and lose money over short periods. For example, when interest rates rise, bond prices fall.

3. Cash and Cash Equivalents. Cash and its equivalents (the category extends to highly liquid, high-quality securities such as one-month Treasury bills) offer low returns over time because they are seen by investors as practically risk-free. Cash may not provide the growth necessary to reach your goals—consider that T-bills have returned just 3.5 percent annually from 1926 through 2013. But cash does add a measure of stability to a portfolio of riskier assets such as stocks and bonds, because cash and cash equivalents rarely decline in value, even over short periods.

A VARIETY OF SUB ASSET CLASSES

In addition to these three main asset classes, there are sub asset classes that contain their own risk and return characteristics. For example:

Equity Sub Asset Classes

Large-Company Stocks
   Large Value Stocks
   Large Growth Stocks

Small-Company Stocks
   Small Value Stocks
   Small Growth Stocks

Real Estate Investment Trusts (REITs)

International Stocks
   Large International Value Stocks
   Large International Growth Stocks
   Small International Value Stocks

Small International Growth Stocks

Emerging Market Stocks (including large and small value and growth)

Fixed Income Sub Asset Classes

Government Bonds

Corporate Bonds

Municipal Bonds

International Bonds

Cash and Cash Equivalents Sub Asset Classes

Treasury Bills

Money Market Securities

Certificates of Deposit

THE IMPORTANCE OF ASSET ALLOCATION

You may not realize how important your asset allocation decisions will be to your future success as an investor. Research has shown that the asset classes you choose and the percentage that you dedicate to each in a broadly diversified portfolio will determine your portfolio's variability and long-term return more than any other factor or decision you make.

The accompanying illustration, The Power of Asset Allocation & Diversification, illustrates this concept by presenting two portfolios. Both consist entirely of equities. But while Portfolio One has just one asset class represented (large US companies found in the S&P 500 index), Portfolio Two is equally divided among four equity subasset classes—domestic, developed international, emerging markets, and real estate. Had you invested in Portfolio One during the fourteen years through 2013, you would have had an annual return of 3.6 percent. A beginning portfolio balance of $1,000,000 would have ended the period with $1,640,241, for a gain of $640,241.

Comparatively, Portfolio Two, with four asset classes, earned a much higher annual rate of return of 7.4 percent and would have ended the period with $2,718,377, for a gain of $1,718,377. The best and worst annual returns for Portfolio 1 were 32.3 percent (2013) and -37 percent (2008). The best and worst annual returns for Portfolio Two were 41.6 percent (2009) and -43.1 percent (2008).

THE POWER OF
ASSET ALLOCATION & DIVERSIFICATION

	PORTFOLIO ONE 100% Equity Portfolio with ONE Asset Class	PORTFOLIO TWO 100% Equity Portfolio with FOUR Asset Classes
Beginning Value 1/10/00	$1,000,000	$1,000,000
Ending Value 12/31/13	$1,640,241	$2,718,377
Annualized Return	3.6%	7.4%
Lowest One Year Return	-37.0% (2008)	-43.1% (2008)
Highest One Year Return	32.3% (2013)	41.6% (2009)

Source: Morningstar. Assumptions: Portfolio One's returns represent total annual returns of the S&P 500® Index. Portfolio Two allocates 25% each to the following indexes: S&P 500, MSCI Emerging Markets, MSCI EAFE, and Dow Jones US Select REIT. Portfolios rebalanced annually. Returns include reinvestment of dividends, interest, and capital gains. Indexes are unmanaged, do not incur fees or expenses, and cannot be invested in directly. Diversification does not eliminate the risk of investment losses. Past performance is no indication of future results. For illustrative purposes only.

The evidence is clear: Focus on getting your portfolio's asset allocation and investment policy the way you want it to be before going further.

UNDERSTAND RISK AND PORTFOLIO STRUCTURE

In order to structure your portfolio with a combination of asset classes necessary to generate your target rate of return, consider the following dimensions of risk and return that have been identified by the academic community:

Equities

1. Market (equity). This dimension of risk tells us that stocks have higher expected returns over time than do fixed income securities such as government bonds. Taking on more market risk in your portfolio—which is accomplished by owning more equities—should result in higher returns. (The data in the following three graphs represent annualized returns over the period from 1928 to 2013.)

RISK & PORTFOLIO STRUCTURE - MARKET EQUITY

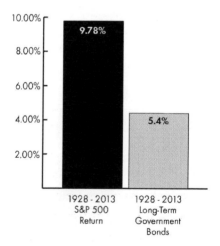

Source: Dimensional Fund Advisors. Indexes are unmanaged, do not incur fees or expenses, and cannot be invested in directly. Diversification does not eliminate the risk of investment losses. Past performance is no indication of future results. For illustrative purposes only.

2. Size. As seen in the accompanying bar graph (Risk & Portfolio Structure – Size), stocks with small market capitalizations (small caps) tend to reward investors over time with better returns than do stocks with large market capitalizations (large caps). The reason, quite simply, is that small companies are riskier than large firms—they tend to have less stable, less consistent financial results from year to year than do large companies.

RISK & PORTFOLIO STRUCTURE - SIZE

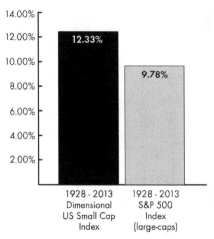

Source: Dimensional Fund Advisors. Indexes are unmanaged, do not incur fees or expenses, and cannot be invested in directly. Diversification does not eliminate the risk of investment losses. Past performance is no indication of future results. For illustrative purposes only.

3. Relative price. Value stocks have been shown to generate stronger returns than growth stocks over time (see the bar graph Risk & Portfolio Structure – Price). The reason, once again, comes down to risk. Value stocks come with more uncertainty about the future of the companies—that's why they are shunned or overlooked by many investors. Because of the uncertainty, investors bid the prices of these companies' shares down—which in turn gives those shares their potential for higher returns in the future if the negative situations at these firms improve.

RISK & PORTFOLIO STRUCTURE - PRICE

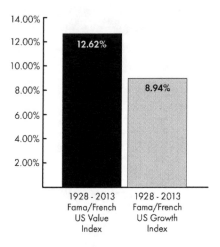

Despite their impressive returns, you would not want to own just these four types of investments. The reason is that no type of asset always performs well. For example, small-cap stocks can lag behind large-cap stocks for many years, while value shares can perform poorly relative to growth shares for extended periods of time. To experience a smoother investment experience and greater peace of mind, your portfolio needs to include a broad range of asset classes.

The upshot: Tilting your portfolio to favor equities, small stocks, and value stocks gives you the potential for stronger returns over time. And while there is no question that this strategy carries risk—your portfolio may experience more ups and downs over shorter periods—it is a risk that has been proven to compensate investors.

Fixed Income

In the fixed income component of a portfolio, we recommend the following subasset classes:

1. Short-term and intermediate-term bonds. The most important role of bonds in a diversified portfolio is to reduce the overall volatility that the stock market component of the portfolio presents. Consider that from January 2000 through December 2009, the S&P 500 index's annual return was -0.9 percent, while bonds (as measured by Barclays US Aggregate Bond Index) had an annual return of 6.3 percent. Bonds help to reduce the risk of a portfolio during periods when stocks decline in value.

Short-term and intermediate-term bonds offer the most attractive balance of return and risk. Long-term bonds (for example, 30-year Treasury bonds) are more sensitive to unexpected changes in interest rates and do not offer enough additional return to compensate for that extra risk.

2. High-quality bonds. Bonds from reliable issuers such as the US government and financially stable companies also can provide a measure of stability to a portfolio. However, like longer-term bonds, lower-quality bonds (for example, those rated below investment grade) offer significantly more risk than high-quality issues—the risk of defaulting on payment, for example—but without a significantly higher return. Once again, investors aren't especially well rewarded for taking on the risks associated with owning lower-quality bonds. For that reason, we suggest you emphasize high-quality holdings in the bond portion of your portfolio.

CHOOSING THE RIGHT MIX OF ASSETS

By now, you know the total rate of return that your investments need to earn over time to reach your goals. With that in mind, consider the potential returns available from various combinations of equities, bonds, and cash (see the accompanying table, Range of Potential Returns for Various Portfolio Combinations).

RANGE OF POTENTIAL RETURNS FOR VARIOUS PORTFOLIO COMBINATIONS

Portfolio Allocation (% equities/ % bonds & cash)	Expected Long-Term Return (annual- ized)	Expected Range of Returns (1-year period)	Expected Range of Returns (3-year period)	Expected Range of Returns (5-year period)
0% / 100%	3.3%	-1.0% to +7.7%	+0.9% to +5.7%	+1.2% to +5.3%
20% / 80%	4.4%	-3.1% to +11.9%	+0.2% to +8.7%	+0.8% to +7.5%
40% / 60%	5.5%	-7.5% to +18.5%	-2.0% to +13.3%	-0.7% to +11.5%
60% / 40%	6.6%	-12.3% to +25.6%	-4.7% to +17.7%	-1.5% to +14.4%
80% / 20%	7.7%	-17.2% to +32.7%	-7.1% to +22.2%	-4.5% to +17.9%
100% / 0%	8.8%	-22.0% to +39.5%	-9.5% to +28.3%	-5.8% to +21.8%

Source: Hatton Consulting, Inc. There is a 2% chance of realizing a return greater than the low and high return above. Please remember that past performance may not be indicative of future results. Different types of investments involve varying degrees of risk, including loss of principal, and there can be no assurance that the future performance of any specific investment or investment strategy will be profitable. Indices are unmanaged baskets of securities in which investors cannot directly invest. Portfolio expected returns and ranges above are for illustrative purposes only.

In the table, we see that a higher allocation to stocks suggests a higher overall potential return. For example, a 100 percent stock portfolio is expected to generate an annual return of 8.8 percent. At first glance, that looks hard to pass up. But also notice how much riskier that all-stock portfolio is compared to the others. For example, the range of potential returns for the all-stock portfolio during a one-year period is anywhere from -22 percent to 39.5 percent. In contrast, the range of returns for the all-bond/cash portfolio is much narrower, at just -1 percent to 7.7 percent. The upshot: The all-stock portfolio is most likely to experience big swings in value over short periods—an experience that most likely would cause a great deal of stress for all but the most risk-averse investors.

Next, look at a portfolio with a balance among stocks, bonds, and cash equivalents, such as the one with a 60 percent allocation to stocks and a 40 percent allocation to fixed income and cash equivalents. That combination can be expected to produce a long-term annual return of 6.6 percent—lower than the all-stock portfolio, but still higher than the historical 3 percent rate of inflation. What's more, it's a less risky portfolio than the all-stock portfolio, as seen by its narrower range of potential returns over one, three, and five years.

Obviously you want to find the asset allocation combination that comes closest to matching your target rate of return. Say, for example, that you require an average annual return of 6.4 percent to reach your goals. You might reasonable opt for the 60 percent stock/40 percent bond and cash portfolio, which is expected to return 6.6 percent annually over time.

DON'T IGNORE YOUR RISK TOLERANCE

That said, it's not quite as simple as picking from a list based on projected return. Keep in mind that risk—and more importantly, your level of tolerance for it—should play a role in your decision. Consider again that 60 percent stock/40 percent bond portfolio, this time with an eye on the lower end of its likely range of returns: -12.3 percent. Ask yourself this question: What would I likely do if my portfolio declined 12.3 percent over a twelve-month period? Would I hold tight?

Add new money when prices were down? Or would I get nervous at seeing such a loss and sell some (or all) of my portfolio?

Before you answer, think about this another way: Say you had a $2 million portfolio, and it fell to $1,754,000 over the course of a year. Would you be able to stay with your allocation and rest easy at night?

If so, you have found a portfolio that is a strong match for you based on both your return goals and your risk tolerance.

If not, you will need to accept a portfolio that delivers lower potential returns in exchange for less volatility over short periods. You'll also need to ask yourself these questions:

1. Can I save more money toward my goals? Socking away more money into your investments can help close the gap. Putting an extra $1,000 per month in investments that earn 5 percent annually will yield an additional $155,282 in ten years.

2. Can I delay my goals? Thanks to compounding, the more time you give your invested capital to grow, the better off you will be. Consider pushing back your retirement for a few years if that's feasible.

3. Can you live on less? Examine your answers from the discovery process about what you need to live on in retirement (and see the Budget Worksheet in chapter 7). Can you make any downward adjustments in any of the categories that lower your income needs?

Select Your Investments

Once you have your framework designed, it's time to fill it in with the specific investment vehicles you will use to meet your asset allocation targets and pursue your desired rate of return.

The best way to accomplish this task is to use mutual funds, which eliminates the task of selecting specific stocks while avoiding others, and offers an efficient and cost-effective way to access entire asset classes based on your asset allocation strategy.

However, with more than 20,000 mutual funds in existence, you need a way to sort through the huge number of choices and select the right funds for you based on both your goals and the fundamentals of the funds themselves.

I recommend an investment rating system called the fi360 Fiduciary Score, which evaluates investments on eleven criteria to determine if they meet a minimum fiduciary standard of care. Using this process will narrow your choices to the top 25 percent of investment vehicles with the highest fiduciary score. You can also use this process to compare investments consistently over time. We use it at Hatton each quarter to test the funds we offer and determine if they still deserve a spot in our lineup.

Determine Your Rebalancing Strategy

Any smart investment plan has a rebalancing strategy—rules that will help you maintain your desired asset allocation.

Rebalancing a portfolio is necessary every now and then. The reason, of course, is that as the financial markets fluctuate, so will the value of your investments. Given enough time, your portfolio will become tilted too far to one type of asset class and not exposed enough to another.

Having a lopsided portfolio can expose you to more risk than you can comfortably tolerate. For example, say stocks soar in value over the next few years, and you find your allocation to stocks has become much higher than your target allocation. While you'd certainly be happy about the big gains you've generated, you would also be overexposed to a segment of the market that could be overvalued and due for a correction. The losses you could experience due to that larger-than-desired exposure to stocks could be severe enough to threaten your chances of reaching your goals on time. Occasional portfolio rebalancing heads off that potential trouble.

In general, you should consider rebalancing a portfolio back to its target allocation when the overall allocation or subasset classes deviate by plus or minus 25 percent from the target. This is just a general rule, however. In practice, there are other factors to consider, including the potential tax impact of any rebalancing. I will explore the nuances of rebalancing in chapter 4.

Add up Your Fees

It's important to understand the costs associated with your investment plan. For one, it's just good sense to know what you are paying. But it's also wise to keep your investment costs low so that more of your returns end up in your wallet and not someone else's.

Typically, there are three primary levels of fees associated with wealth management:

- **Asset management fees.** These are fees that are charged by your investments, such as your mutual funds. For example, each fund charges an expense ratio that pays for the fund's management, accounting, and legal fees, and recordkeeping. You can compare the expense ratios of various funds you are considering by using a service such as Morningstar (morningstar.com).
- **Custodial/transaction fees.** These are fees incurred when you (or your advisor) buy and sell securities through a custodian (such as Schwab).
- **Advisory fees.** This is the fee an advisor charges for managing the wealth management process—including creating and managing your personal wealth management plan, accounting, monitoring, and reporting. When evaluating financial

advisors, check their fees and ask for a detailed description of what they offer for that price.

Document It All

You're almost finished. The final step of developing an investment plan is to write down all of the information you have gathered into a formal document, called an Investment Policy Statement (IPS). This will be one of the most powerful tools in your investment toolkit.

An IPS is a written reminder of every key element that goes into your wealth management plan—from your goals and values to your time horizon and risk tolerance to the specific details of the investment strategy you have outlined for yourself. When you put all of this information on paper, you will find that you have tremendous clarity about the reasons behind why and how you are investing.

That clarity will come in handy if you find yourself wanting to make changes to your plan that may not be in your best interest. Say, for example, that stocks have been on a tear recently, and the headlines in the media are screaming about all the new record highs that the major indexes are hitting each week. In that environment, it's easy to start feeling euphoric about stocks and wondering if you shouldn't significantly boost your exposure. Likewise, there may be times when short-term declines or extended periods of losses in the market make you nervous and tempt you to flee from stocks. Your IPS is designed to protect you from making those rash, emotional decisions. It serves as a constant, written reminder of the strategy you have put in place for your investments and, just as important, the reasons behind that strategy. Any time you consider making a change to your strategy, first review your IPS to see if such a change makes sense—and if your idea is being driven by logic or by emotion.

For a detailed look at what information should go into your IPS and what a typical IPS looks like at Hatton Consulting, go to chapter 8.

It's Time to Commit

You're now ready to take the next crucial step on your path to a successful wealth management experience: Committing to your plan and putting it in motion so it can start working hard for you. That's what we'll cover in the next chapter.

CHAPTER 3

Make Your Commitment and Implement Your Plan: The Third Step to a Secure and Meaningful Financial Life

The next part of the wealth management process is important, yet easy to overlook or undervalue: Committing to your investment plan and taking the steps required to put it into motion so your assets begin working for you as they should.

The straightforward nature of these steps means we don't need to spend a great deal of time on them in this book. (As you will see, this is its shortest chapter.) That said, you'll find it helpful to understand what happens at this stage.

DEALING WITH THE DOCUMENTS

The most important task in this step is to sign the paperwork that will enable you to implement your plan. At Hatton Consulting, for example, new clients execute documents to transfer assets from their existing custodian to the custodian we use.

When filling out these documents, it is important to pay close attention to a few pieces of information so that all the *i*s are dotted and the *t*s are crossed. The following issues should be reviewed and addressed if needed:

1. Titling of assets. How you title your assets will play a role in how they are taxed, who has control of the assets while you are living and after you pass, and how those assets are transferred at death. The option or options you choose will determine things such as whether your assets go through probate, their cost basis at the time they are transferred, and the rules governing who is allowed to sell or transfer the property.

2. Consolidation. If you have multiple IRAs, SEP IRAs, and 401(k)s and other tax-deferred retirement vehicles, it almost certainly makes sense to consolidate them into the fewest accounts necessary. Doing so helps reduce your costs of investing and makes it easier to manage the assets to conform to your investment plan. This is the stage at which duplicative accounts start getting consolidated.

3. Beneficiary designations. You want your assets to go the people, charities, or trusts of your choosing when the time comes. When you name a beneficiary on an investment account, those assets can pass directly to whomever you designate—enabling you to skip probate, a potentially expensive legal process that you want to avoid if at all possible. If you do not name a beneficiary, it is extremely likely that your assets will go through probate. What's more, beneficiary designations will override your will.

When you commit to a new plan, take the time to review the designations on each account to ensure that they are still relevant. Changes in our lives—marriages, births, deaths—can make existing beneficiary designations out of date and in need of revision. Outdated beneficiary designations (like older parents or ex-spouses) could lead to unintended outcomes for your wealth and family.

REVIEWING CORE CONCEPTS

The implementation of your investment plan is also a great opportunity to remind yourself of your investment philosophy, the central tenets of your plan, and the importance of staying committed to those tenets post-launch.

As you are well aware, there is no shortage of noise when it comes to your investments—and you can be sure that shortly after you implement your plan, you will run across an opinion that flies in the face of your strategy. In such cases, remind yourself that the advice that gets bandied about in the media (or at parties, book clubs, or other social engagements) should be viewed as nothing more than entertainment. To see what I mean, search the Internet for old year-end review articles with experts predicting what will happen in the coming year with the financial markets. You'll be amazed at how many of those prognosticators were flat-out wrong. Your focus should remain on making wise financial decisions and sticking with your long-term plan.

Also keep in mind that reaching your goals will not be a straight-line path from point A to point B. Investment gains tend to be concentrated during relatively short periods. You have to stay committed to your plan to capture those gains. If you get off track, it is bound to cost you.

SOME COMMON QUESTIONS

When I take new clients through this stage of the process, certain questions tend to come up more than others.

For example, clients may have questions about some of their holdings from previous accounts. Say that your new investment plan requires that you sell some older holdings that you have owned for years (or even decades). You might feel somewhat uncomfortable about selling, even though you are on board with your new investment plan. In that case, we might consider selling those holdings slowly, over a period of months or years. Conversely, we might keep some or all of those holdings but transfer them to a separate account so that they are no longer part of your primary investment portfolio.

A related issue that gets discussed often involves the possibility of generating a hefty tax bill if existing assets are sold to make way for new investments. In cases where a sale would trigger a significant capital gains liability, we recommend transferring the assets "in kind" from the old account to the new account. This approach simply moves the assets and does not involve any selling. Once transferred, the sale of the assets can be timed in ways that minimize or eliminate taxable events. Other strategies can be used as well, such as offsetting realized gains with realized losses from other investments.

Another common question comes up when retired clients take monthly distributions from their current accounts to fund their expenses. The timing of any account transfer needs to be managed so that those distributions are not disrupted. At our firm, knowing that transfers take approximately fourteen days, we schedule them to be completed before the next distribution.

Of course, you may have further questions or want to discuss different concerns. Each implementation meeting is designed to address any issues that are on your mind that you need to answer before committing to your plan.

THE RESULT: A GREATER LEVEL OF COMFORT

By the end of this relatively short part of the consultative wealth management process, you will have great confidence in the road ahead. What may have been a mishmash of multiple investment accounts is streamlined and simplified—giving you more clarity about your financial situation than you may have ever had before.

Now that you are launched, it's time to dig a bit deeper into some of your noninvestment challenges and opportunities. You'll also want to track your progress to ensure that your plan is doing what it's supposed to. In the next chapter, we'll take a close look at advanced-level planning and regular progress meetings. As you will see, these two components will play major roles in helping you achieve your goals.

CHAPTER 4

Checking In: Regular Progress Meetings and the Importance of Advanced Planning

As you move forward on your journey toward achieving your financial goals, it is important to assess your progress now and again to determine if you are still on the right course—and to decide if anything important in your life has changed that would require you to revisit your plan and make changes.

At Hatton Consulting, we schedule regular progress meetings to compare actual results to stated goals. At these meetings, we also introduce and implement one of the signal aspects of superior wealth management: *planning at an advanced level* to address all the investment and noninvestment issues that face investors with significant wealth.

What follows is an overview of how we conduct these regular progress meetings. If you work with us at Hatton, this overview will give you a good idea of the "look and feel" of this part of the process. If you choose to manage your own wealth independently, you'll come away with some guidelines about how to conduct self-assessments on your own.

CONDUCTING AN INVESTMENT REVIEW

The first step is to look back over your financial and personal goals to see whether there have been any changes to your personal or financial situation. New developments in your life—such as changes in your marital status, the birth or death of family members, or an unexpected inheritance—can impact your existing goals and financial status. That, in turn, can affect the level of investment risk you can comfortably tolerate, as well as the target rate of return you require to meet your goals. When that happens, changes may need to be made to your portfolio, typically in your allocations among asset classes. If your financial and personal goals haven't changed since your last meeting, we simply review your progress with you to see how you are faring in each area.

Next, review the asset allocation of your portfolio and the expected annual rate of return of that mix, which will be documented on your investment policy statement, and compare it to your portfolio's actual performance to see if your investments are meeting expectations. For example, say you invested in a portfolio with a 40 percent equity allocation and a 60 percent bond allocation. That portfolio might have an expected annualized return over the long term of 5.4 percent. It also might be reasonably expected to gain as much as nearly 19 percent or decline as much as -8 percent during any one-year period. There is also the possibility, albeit slim (about a 2 percent chance), that this portfolio could decline more than 8 percent during a one-year period. Compare those expected results with the results you earned during the past year (as well as your results over longer periods such as three years, five years, ten years, and since inception) to determine if your portfolio is behaving as it should.

Occasionally, the performance of the financial markets and your investments will cause your portfolio's asset allocation to drift away from its intended targets. If the stock market soars for an extended period, for example, you may find that you now own more stock investments than you wish to own, based on your investment policy statement. Conversely, a bad year for stocks might leave your portfolio with a lower exposure to stocks than you want.

When those moments occur, it may be time to rebalance your portfolio back to the intended target mix. Common rebalancing strategies include the following:

1. Rebalancing when a particular asset class is above or below its target value by a certain percentage (such as 25 percent). For example, say that your target allocation to large US value stocks is 10 percent of your overall portfolio. You would look to add to those stocks when your actual allocation falls below 7.5 percent, and you would look to sell when it rises above 12.5 percent (see the accompanying table, "Asset Class Rebalancing"). By doing so, you maintain the risk and return profile that you have determined is right for you, and your portfolio maintains the characteristics that will help it deliver the type of returns you seek over time.

ASSET CLASS REBALANCING

Asset Class	Target Allocation	Sell when above	Buy when below
Large-Cap Value	10%	12.5%	7.5%
Small-Cap Blend	8%	10%	6%

2. Rebalancing at a specific time or frequency, such as once every six months or once every year (often in December before the end of the calendar year). This approach helps ensure that rebalancing occurs on a consistent basis over time.

3. Rebalancing when cash is added to, or withdrawn from, the portfolio. New cash being added would be invested in the asset class (or classes, as the case may be) that is farthest below its target allocation at the time the cash is deposited. If cash needs to be withdrawn from the portfolio (for example, to pay for an unintended retirement expense), investments from the asset class that is farthest above its target would be sold (assuming no negative tax impact from the sale) in order to maintain the intended overall portfolio allocation.

If you fail to rebalance, you expose yourself to unnecessary risks that could potentially derail your plan. You might, for example, be too exposed to stocks at a moment when stock prices plummet. Or you might not own enough stocks during a period when stock prices rise fast and miss out on gains. Determining whether the portfolio needs to be rebalanced is a crucial step in the regular progress meeting process.

IMPLEMENTING ADVANCED PLANNING STRATEGIES

Regular progress meetings are also when we review strategies for meeting investors' planning needs.

As you recall from this book's introduction, advanced-level planning is one of the three chief components of comprehensive wealth management as we practice it. Broadly, advanced planning develops strategies to help individuals and families with noninvestment concerns that they face and coordinates those strategies with investment consulting decisions.

Advanced planning falls into five main areas. Each will be covered in detail in later chapters. For now, this list should give you a good overview of what advanced planning is and why it's so useful in comprehensive wealth management.

1. Tax planning. This component seeks to minimize the impact of taxes on your investment returns and your overall income. The following topics frequently come up during regular progress meetings:

- offsetting any realized gains by harvesting losses from elsewhere in the portfolio
- withdrawal strategies for retirement income, including which accounts (trusts, Roth IRAs, annuities, and stocks with various cost bases) should be tapped first to pay for current expenses, and which should remain untouched until a later date
- areas of your financial life other than investments that affect taxation (such as business interests, or passive interest from property) and how to be tax-efficient in those areas.

2. Estate planning and wealth transfer. Here, you're after the most tax-efficient ways to pass assets to succeeding generations, based on your wishes. Some goals of wealth transfer include deciding the best ways for your assets to be gifted to family members during your lifetime or distributed at death or incapacity, determining how and when your heirs will receive money, and ensuring that the maximum amount possible is transferred while minimizing taxes—all accomplished as efficiently and with as few headaches as possible. Common wealth transfer topics of discussion include

- determining what documents you already have and what others you may still need or need to update (for example, a will, a trust, or medical directives),
- setting rules for what will happen with your assets if you become incapacitated and what happens when you die,

- the estate tax implications of those plans,
- selecting an executor and/or trustee, and
- ensuring that heirs have access to appropriate amounts of cash to fund final arrangements and pay immediate expenses.

3. Insurance planning. The ability to protect yourself and those you care about from many of the risks in the world is absolutely vital to your financial well-being and your peace of mind. Insurance can play a decisive role in providing that protection. Conversations about insurance planning often focus on these issues:

- Figuring out what risks you and your family face (or could face going forward). Categories of risk may include short- and long-term disability, long-term health care, and death.
- Formulating an appropriate response to those risks—which might include retaining the risk yourself, transferring the risk through insurance, or combining those approaches.
- Your existing coverage in terms of life insurance, long-term care insurance, umbrella protection, and other policies. Do you have the right types of insurance and the appropriate amount of coverage?

4. Asset protection. These strategies shield your wealth from litigants and creditors so that your assets are not unjustly taken from you. Asset protection discussions often focus on these issues:

- The risks you face or potentially could face in your career and personal life. Are you a physician or a business owner who could be sued, for example? Are you a pilot, or do you ride a motorcycle? Do you travel frequently, especially to countries that may be less welcoming to Americans?

- The level of asset protection, if any, that you already enjoy through your existing investments. In our state of Arizona, for example, IRAs are protected from creditors, as is the first $150,000 of the value of your personal residence.

5. Charitable giving. There are ways to maximize the effectiveness of any charitable intent you might have—enabling gifts that are far greater than what would have been possible otherwise. Here we evaluate the options for giving and how they affect or complement strategies for your retirement income and wealth transfer goals. Conversations about charitable and philanthropic goals often include discussions about the following:

- identifying charities or nonprofits (such as a church, hospital, alma mater, or social service organization) that you wish to support
- any existing gifting you do, and the effectiveness of that gifting from a tax perspective
- gifting options to consider, such as donor-advised funds and various types of charitable trusts, based on your goals and the tax advantages of each option
- identifying ways to maximize gifts, such as donating highly appreciated assets to avoid realized gains

A CONTINUING AND INTEGRATED PROCESS OVER TIME

As you will probably guess by now, none of these areas stands apart from the rest. For example, wealth protection is often intertwined with wealth transfer. That's why it's important to deal with each area systematically while maintaining an integrated approach that never loses sight of your overall financial picture.

Regular progress meetings are designed with all this in mind. Depending on your needs at a given moment in time, and the most desirable goals on the horizon, these meetings may cover a range of planning issues, or they may focus on one at a time. Other professionals that you work with, such as accountants and attorneys, can be brought into these meetings whenever that's helpful.

The upshot: Regular progress meetings are a reality check. They allow you to see where you've been and where you are today, and to make sure the road ahead is clear. Armed with that information, you can continue to make astute decisions about your wealth—and ensure that every strategy you're using reflects what you want for yourself, your family, and perhaps even the world at large at every step of the way.

CHAPTER 5

Putting Wealth Management
to Work: A Case Study

At this point, you should have a reasonably strong understanding of what wealth management means and the components it should include. Now it's time to tie those components together so you can see how wealth management works in real life—on the ground, as it were.

To do that, consider the case of a couple who first came to see me in 2005. As you read, notice how many of the elements of wealth management, covered in previous chapters, were brought to bear on their situation in an integrated, coordinated manner. You'll see how decisions made in one area of their finances reflect other aspects of their lives. While this couple's circumstances are unique, you are likely to see similarities in your own situation.

BOB AND SHERRY: FROM CONFUSION TO CLARITY

Bob and Sherry were co-owners of a thriving manufacturing business. Bob was the "hands-on" partner who oversaw daily operations; Sherry managed the administrative responsibilities, including the financials.

The couple had accumulated substantial assets over the years. But as with many successful entrepreneurs, business considerations typically took precedence over their personal finances. Sherry was justifiably proud of her financial acumen but had reached a point where the scope and complexity of their business and personal finances were beginning to overwhelm her. She was hesitant to make decisions for fear she might do something counterproductive or, worse, trigger a negative tax consequence if she sold, moved, or consolidated part of their assets. She desperately wanted to organize and simplify their life and spend less time managing the finances. It was this sense of frustration that finally convinced Sherry to seek professional help from a wealth manager.

Bob and Sherry were in their mid-fifties when they came to see me. They had been married for thirty years (the second marriage for each). Each had a child from a first marriage: One was a financially independent professional; the other had special needs. All four of the couple's parents were deceased.

We began by developing a list of their personal goals and values, which included simplifying the management of their financial life, living an independent and financially secure retirement, and not being a burden to their children during their old age or in the event of incapacity or disability.

As for their financial status, the couple had $2.6 million in investable assets, plus their business real estate valued at $1.5 million. They owned two mortgaged homes with combined equity of about $600,000.

Their investments were spread across five different financial and banking institutions in nineteen different accounts, including investment, checking, savings, IRA, Roth, profit sharing, and annuity accounts. There was no coordination among these, and—not surprisingly—hey found the nineteen monthly statements from different custodians confusing. Often, months would pass before they would open various statements.

Because of this multiplicity of financial institutions and accounts, diversification and rebalancing strategies were either nonexistent or significantly compromised. Many of their accounts were invested in similar asset classes. So while the couple thought they were adequately diversified because they owned a variety of mutual funds, my review revealed that many of the mutual funds owned the same companies. The couple was not properly diversified at all. They also were uncertain as to which accounts to tap for distribution should they need income from the portfolio.

Their finances, once we laid them out, were characterized by a glaring lack of overall clarity. For example, investment management fees were complex and confusing (again due to the nineteen distinct accounts). Some accounts were commission-oriented, making charges hard to track. Other types of fees were just as difficult to determine because they were not transparent. There were no comprehensive investment performance reports, so they had no way to compute the overall rate of return on the combined portfolio or its performance on an after-fee basis compared to benchmark portfolios. That meant the couple, who had made so many individual investment decisions over the years, could not be certain if they were earning the return they needed to achieve their goals.

Similarly, there was no effective tax planning strategy. Four conditions increased Bob and Sherry's tax liability:

- There was no strategy to offset realized gains with realized losses.
- Their state tax liability was elevated because their municipal bond holdings were not state tax favored.
- They had health care-related expenses that were not tax deductible.
- Their potential estate tax liability exposure had not been addressed.

There were also gaps in the couple's estate plan and asset protection plan. For example, Sherry was an amateur pilot. What would happen to the couple's combined assets if she crashed? There were two trusts—a family trust and an irrevocable life insurance trust—and multiple insurance policies from five different carriers. They thought they were adequately covered. But there was no umbrella policy to protect their assets against potential lawsuits.

Even though the couple had engaged several advisors, there was no coordinated strategy among the investment and insurance professionals, custodians, and tax or estate planning attorneys. No one seemed to be talking to anyone else.

Little wonder Sherry was immobilized and exhausted.

After gathering all this information from our discovery meeting with Bob and Sherry, we analyzed their situation. It was apparent they needed guidance to help them get better organized, rationalize their financial situation, and simplify their lives.

INVESTMENT PLANNING

The first step was to create a profile of the couple's financial situation. We reviewed all their expenses and determined how much income they would need annually in retirement. Next, we subtracted existing pension and Social Security income to arrive at the amount of money needed from their portfolio to meet their annual expenses. Once we had that number, we were able to determine an appropriate asset allocation. In the accompanying example, titled Investment Planning, we calculate the investment return needed to generate the retirement income Bob and Sherry require: 4.81 percent, which called for a recommended asset allocation of 30 percent stocks and 70 percent fixed income and cash.

INVESTMENT PLANNING

EXPENSES AND INCOME SOURCES	AMOUNT
Total Annual Expenses	$104,000
Taxes (20%)	$26,000
Gross Income Needed	**$130,000**
Less: Annual Social Security Income	($26,000)
Less: Rental Income from Commercial Real Estate	($32,000)
Less: Annual Pension Income	($25,000)
Income Needed from Portfolio	**$47,000**
Target Rate of Return without Inflation Adjustment (portfolio income needed, divided by portfolio total)	$47,000/$2,600,000=1.81%
Target rate of return + inflation adjustment (3%)	1.81% + 3.0% = 4.81%
Recommended Asset Allocation to Achieve Investment Return of 4.81%	30% stock allocation / 70% fixed income allocation

Next, we evaluated their existing investments by asset class, performance, tax status, and several other considerations. This enabled us to consolidate their nineteen accounts down to just five, with one custodian and one bank, alleviating the mountain of monthly statements. We then reached out to their tax advisor and worked together to identify taxable gains within the portfolio and offset them with unrealized losses, including losses within their business that could be used to offset gains. This allowed us to liquidate undesirable investments and consolidate the accounts without creating any tax liability for Bob and Sherry.

We drafted all this into a formal investment policy statement (IPS). Information contained in their IPS included the following:

- list of all their financial assets
- family, legacy, and financial goals
- retirement income needed
- sources of income (e.g., Social Security, pension, rent)
- tax data
- target rate of return required from portfolio to meet income needed
- asset allocation
- investment selection criteria
- list of selected investments
- rebalancing guidelines
- contact information for all their professional advisors
- executors' and trustees' names and contact information
- calculation of investment management fees

A concise document by design, the IPS showed Bob and Sherry a high-definition picture of where they were and what they needed to know to make informed choices moving forward.

ONGOING TAX PLANNING

Once Bob and Sherry reviewed the IPS and agreed with the actions proposed, we continued our work with their CPA and their attorney, comparing notes and coordinating our strategy to minimize federal, state, and estate tax liability. Knowing what their tax liability would be was a huge relief for Bob and Sherry. Previously, trying to forecast tax liability with nineteen separate accounts and no communication among advisors was almost impossible.

The coordinated strategy worked. Bob and Sherry were able to maximize after-tax returns. An additional benefit was being able to make maximum contributions to their IRAs and other tax-friendly accounts. It also allowed the couple to run their long-term care policies and health insurance policies through various business entities that were set up, which let them deduct many health care-related expenses that had previously been nondeductible.

ESTATE PLANNING

After the investment and tax planning strategies were implemented, we met with Bob and Sherry and their attorney, tax advisor, and trustee to address their estate planning goals. We adjusted and reinforced the trust documents to align with their goals: meeting their retirement needs while living, managing their assets if they became incapacitated, and having a seamless wealth transfer to their children.

We helped them spell out what would happen if they were involved in an automobile accident and both were incapacitated for a few months—who they would want to help pay their bills, make sure their special-needs child was taken care of, and keep their affairs rolling whether their injuries were a short- or long-term event. There were provisions to ensure that the services being delivered to their special-needs child would not be impacted.

INSURANCE PLANNING

The next step in the process was to review and coordinate Bob and Sherry's various policies with their insurance professionals. We audited the existing policies to determine if they were sound, well funded, properly titled, and suitable for the duration of the couple's needs. We also confirmed appropriate beneficiary designations.

Last, we conducted a competitive search for an appropriate long-term care planning and funding strategy, and we managed the financial resources intended to fund the various insurance policies.

BOTTOM-LINE BENEFITS

As a result of all these efforts, put in place and updated over a period of several years, Bob and Sherry were able to pay off their two mortgages (substantially reducing their income needs), sell their business assets, and retire with no debt whatsoever. They have a clear picture of their financial situation, and they are reassured by what they see. Their lives have been simplified, and they feel much better organized as they enjoy their well-earned—and well-planned—retirement.

PART TWO

The Wealth Management Experience

CHAPTER 6

Sources of Retirement Income:
A Closer Look at Your Options

As discussed in chapter 1, an essential part of the wealth management process is identifying your sources of retirement income. This is a common element in every retirement plan. The purpose of this chapter is to expand your knowledge of various income sources and offer you some ideas to consider when you look at your own situation.

INCOME SOURCE #1: SOCIAL SECURITY

Social Security is the retirement income source that most investors think of first, and it's no wonder: Social Security accounts for 45 percent or more of the postwork income for roughly 80 percent of retirees.[2] Even affluent Americans receive the benefit of Social Security payments to bridge the gap between their retirement living expenses and what they can draw down from their own resources.

Eligibility

Retirees become eligible for benefits once they earn forty credits. To earn one credit, you must meet a minimum earnings amount, which usually increases each year (check with the Social Security Administration to confirm the current minimum earnings amount). You can earn a maximum of four credits per year. Most people need forty credits to qualify for benefits (generally speaking, this translates to ten years of work). Benefit calculations are based on your lifetime income, with the thirty-five highest years creating the average. A formula is applied to the earnings to determine the benefit amount.

Social Security eligibility starts at age sixty-two, but benefits are reduced for each month prior to your full retirement age. Postponing retirement until age seventy increases the amount of the monthly benefit. So let's say your full retirement age is sixty-six and your monthly benefit at that age is $1,000. If you choose to start receiving benefits at age sixty-two, your monthly benefit will be reduced by 25 percent, to $750. This is generally a permanent reduction in your monthly benefit.

If you choose to wait until age seventy to receive benefits, however, your monthly benefit would increase to $1,320 (or 32 percent more per month than if you chose to start benefits at your full retirement age of 66).[3] Benefits increase 8 percent annually each year between ages sixty-six and seventy (for retirees born in 1943 or after).

The accompanying chart shows eligibility to receive full retirement benefits.

ELIGIBILITY

YEAR OF BIRTH	FULL RETIREMENT AGE
1937 and Prior	65
1938	65 and 2 months
1939	65 and 4 months
1940	65 and 6 months
1941	65 and 8 months
1942	65 and 10 months
1943-1954	66
1955	66 and 2 months
1956	66 and 4 months
1957	66 and 6 months
1958	66 and 8 months
1959	66 and 10 months
1960 or later	67

Source: Social Security Administration

There are some nuances to these rules, however. If you have a spouse, his or her benefits will have an impact on your Social Security income. If a higher-earning spouse delays taking benefits and passes away, for example, the surviving spouse will receive the deceased spouse's benefit, which will be higher.

What's more, widows and widowers can begin receiving Social Security benefits at age sixty (or at age fifty if they are disabled). They can take a reduced benefit on one work-history record and later switch to a full benefit on the other record. For example, a woman could take a reduced widow's benefit at age sixty and then switch to her full retirement benefit when she reaches full retirement age. These rules vary, so you should consult a Social Security representative about available options.

Benefits for family members also exist, including

- spouses age sixty-two or older,
- spouses younger than age sixty-two who are taking care of a younger or disabled child, based on their work-history record,
- divorced spouses age sixty-two or older, assuming their marriage lasted ten years and they are unmarried,
- children up to age eighteen (or nineteen if they are full-time students who have not yet graduated from high school), and
- disabled children age eighteen or older.

You should know that if you are age sixty-two or older and choose to activate your benefits while you are still working, your benefits may be reduced based on your earnings during the year. If you earn over a certain threshold from age sixty-two through age sixty-five, for example, your benefits may be reduced by one dollar for every two dollars in earnings. And in the year you achieve your full retirement age, your benefits may be reduced by one dollar for every three dollars in earnings. The thresholds for these reductions change each year. For up-to-date information on how earnings affect your retirement benefits, see the Social Security Administration publication called *How Work Affects Your Benefits*, which contains current annual and monthly earnings limits.

Considerations before Activating Social Security Benefits

- **Taxes.** Only half of Social Security benefits are taxable for couples earning $32,000 to $44,000 and for individuals earning $25,000 to $43,000. For couples earning over $44,000 and individuals over $34,000, 85 percent of the benefits are subject to income tax. Earnings levels are subject to change, so check with a Social Security representative to determine if your current income levels will trigger a taxable event.

- **Cash flow.** If you want to retire at age sixty-two but need additional cash flow to sustain your income, taking benefits early probably makes sense. If your other sources of income—such as a pension, an annuity, or an investment portfolio—are sufficient to meet your cash flow needs, you may want to delay taking benefits until your full retirement age or later. Because benefits grow by 8 percent annually between the ages of sixty-six and seventy (for those born in 1943 or after), retirees who need the additional income may find they are better off tapping into their portfolio and delaying taking benefits.

- **Life expectancy.** Average life expectancy at birth is about seventy-five for men and eighty-one for women. If you reach age sixty-five, however, life expectancy increases to 84.3 and 86.6 for men and women, respectively.[4]

Based on your life expectancy, you can calculate your breakeven age—that is, the age at which you start being financially ahead by having delayed your Social Security benefits. For example, let's say that you are a top wage earner turning sixty-two this year. Your benefits in today's dollars are $1,923 a month at age sixty-two, $2,591 at age sixty-six (your full retirement age), and $3,447 at age seventy (the year when your monthly benefit would reach its maximum amount). Your breakeven ages are:

BREAK-EVEN AGES

Retirement Age	Break Even Age
62 - versus - 66	77 – 78
62 - versus - 70	80 – 81
66 - versus - 70	82 – 82

Source: Hatton Consulting, Inc.

You can see that if you wait until age sixty-six to take Social Security instead of taking it at age sixty-two, you'll come out ahead as long as you live to at least age seventy-seven.

This exercise can be useful. If you have any reason to think you may have a short life expectancy, it might make sense to take your benefits earlier in life rather than later so you have more years in which you will receive benefits. However, if you expect to live longer than your official life expectancy age, it might be smart to hold off and activate benefits later so you receive a higher payout throughout the rest of your long life.

Strategies for Taking Social Security Benefits

There are a variety of ways to take Social Security, based on your age, financial circumstances, and other considerations. Keep in mind, rules and laws dealing with Social Security can significantly change, reduce or eliminate certain strategies. Always check to see if your claiming strategy remains an option and applicable to your situation. Below are two strategies as examples, based on situations I've encountered at my firm:

- **File and suspend.** A healthy married couple believes they will beat the average life expectancy, so they delay filing for benefits until full retirement age (in their case, age sixty-six). The husband earns a substantially higher income than does his wife—entitling him to commensurately higher Social Security benefits. At the time of filing, the higher-earner husband "files and suspends" his benefits until age seventy. This enables his lower-earning spouse to activate her benefit off his work-history record and receive benefits at the time of filing. Meanwhile, the husband continues accumulating delayed retirement credits. At age seventy, he files for his benefit and receives a higher payout.

- **File and restrict.** Here, a husband can claim spousal benefits based on his wife's work-history record and then, at age seventy, switch back to his own higher benefit. That way, two checks are coming in during the interim period.

Note that in these two cases, the record holder (the husband) must wait until full retirement age to file. Any earlier application will void the use of these options.

If you decide to take reduced benefits early and later change your mind, the Social Security Administration will allow you to pay back benefits if the claim is withdrawn within one year of the filing. You can then restart benefits at a later time at a higher payout.

If you plan to delay receiving benefits because you are working, you should sign up for Medicare three months before reaching age sixty-five, regardless of when you reach full retirement age. Otherwise, your Medicare medical insurance could be delayed, and you could be charged higher premiums.

You can estimate benefit amounts and find more information to help you decide when to start receiving retirement benefits by using the Benefits Planners online at www.socialsecurity.gov/planners. You also can use the Retirement Estimator at www.socialsecurity.gov/estimator or create an account and get your Social Security Statement at www.socialsecurity.gov/mystatement. Both provide retirement benefit estimates based on your actual earnings record.

INCOME SOURCE #2: PENSION INCOME AND OPTIONS

A pension plan is a retirement benefit funded in whole or in part by an employer, which pays an annuity payment to a qualifying employee upon retirement. The American Express Co. established the first private pension plan in 1875. Today, millions of Americans receive some form of pension from their employers.

Different pension plans offer different payout options, which can include a lump sum payment, a single life annuity (SLA), a variety of joint and survivor (JS) payments, and ten-year certain and life. Your first step should be to request a formal pension estimate from your employer, to understand the options offered by your pension plan and their potential impact on your retirement plans.

- *Lump sum payment.* Getting your pension payout all at once instead of spread out over time can offer you a high degree of choice and flexibility. You can decide how to invest the lump sum, for example, and spend it when and how you wish. You also can roll it directly into an IRA to avoid paying taxes on the payout. That said, a lump sum also comes with greater responsibility on your part. By taking control of the entire amount, it's up to you to ensure that your money is invested well and lasts throughout your retirement (and perhaps beyond).
- *Single life annuity.* The SLA has the largest payout because it is meant to last only throughout your lifetime and no one

else's. Therefore, retirees often gravitate toward it. But it is important to conduct a "What if?" scenario to ensure the optimal choice based on your portfolio and financial circumstances. For example, if it's likely that your spouse will need payments from your pension to fund his or her expenses after you are gone, an SLA would not be the best choice.

- *Joint and survivor payments.* This option assumes that your spouse will need to keep getting monthly payments from your pension after you are deceased. Naturally, this option pays less than a single-life annuity, because it needs to last for a longer time—your lifetime *and* the life of your spouse.

The JS option typically includes 50, 75, and 100 percent joint and survivor payments. For example a 50 percent JS provides a monthly payment during the primary pensioner's lifetime. Upon death, the spouse continues to receive 50 percent of the original amount until his or her death.

PAYOUT OPTIONS

Payout Option	Primary Pensioner	Survivor Payout
Lump Sum	Entire balance paid out in one check.	$0
Single Life Annuity	$1,200	$0
Joint & 50% Survivor Annuity	$1,000	$500
Joint & 75% Survivor Annuity	$900	$675
Joint & 100% Survivor Annuity	$800	$800
10 Year Certain & Life	$1,100	$1,100

- **Ten Year Certain and Life.** With this option, you receive an annual payout for the rest of your life. If you die during the "period certain" phase (in this example, within ten years after you first start receiving payments), a surviving beneficiary would receive your annual payments until the end of that period. However, your beneficiary would not receive any payments from this type of plan if you die *after* that ten-year period ends.

The upshot on pension benefits: It is vital to conduct a comparative analysis of the payout options, regardless of one's personal situation. In the case of a married couple, the analysis should also include a benefit comparison between both spouses living a full life expectancy, and one spouse not. Here the appropriate option would likely depend on the cash flow needed should one spouse die earlier than expected.

Another consideration is the future stability of your pension plan. Under federal law, all traditional pension plans must report how well they are funded. Pension beneficiaries receive an annual funding notice that reports plan assets and liabilities and the funded percentage.* In general, the higher this percentage, the better funded the plan. You should receive this notice every year. Make sure you review it. It provides an overview of your plan's funding health.

Your plan's funding may guide your payout choice. Example: The plan may offer some attractive annuity payouts, but if you are not comfortable with your plan's stability, you may want to opt for a lump sum payout.

In general, anyone with a spouse should seriously consider a survivor benefit. The question here is what happens to the spouse if the primary pensioner dies earlier than expected. What would loss of a

---

* Under federal law, the plan must report how well it is funded by using a measure called the "funded percentage." This percentage is obtained by dividing the plan's assets by its liabilities on the valuation date for the plan year. Thus, if a pension plan has plan assets of $950,000 and has $1,000,000 in liabilities, it is 95 percent funded.

pension payment do to your family's financial resources? Is there life insurance, and if so, is it adequate to offset a reduced or lost pension payment? If term life insurance is involved, is the term long enough to cover the life expectancy of the primary pensioner? And is the life insurance provider well funded?

A side note: Some retirees question whether the payout disparity between the SLA and JS options is sufficient to justify selecting the SLA and then purchasing a life insurance policy to provide a death benefit should the retiree die prematurely. The beneficiary can invest the death benefit to replace the lost income associated with the SLA. This strategy is always worth considering. However, in my experience, it usually is not the best option. Typically, the cost of the insurance policy is prohibitive, the insurance company is unwilling to issue a lengthy enough policy because of the advanced age of the retiree, or the difference between the SLA and a survivor annuity is not enough to fund the cost of a life insurance policy.

INCOME SOURCE #3: RENTAL INCOME

If you receive rental income from commercial or residential property, you must decide if you want to continue being a landlord in retirement. You also must watch out for common errors when calculating rental income, such as mistaking gross income for net income. Even if any debt has been paid down and the property is generating positive cash flow, expenses must be accounted for. General maintenance and upkeep, property taxes, management fees, turnover, and HOA fees (in the case of residential property) all must be deducted to arrive at an accurate net income figure.

INCOME SOURCE #4: OTHER PASSIVE INCOME

Passive interests from business activity is another source of retirement income for some investors. One couple I worked with decided to sell their manufacturing business to their employee. In addition to the real estate and physical manufacturing plant, there was a great deal of specialized machinery and equipment. The employees did not have the financial resources to fund the entire purchase, so the sellers negotiated a ten-year buyout that included substantial passive rental income, which enhanced their cash flow early on in their retirement and lowered their taxes by doling out the income over time.

INCOME SOURCE #5: DEFERRED COMPENSATION PLANS

These plans are often used by executives earning high incomes, as a supplement to more traditional workplace retirement saving options such as 401(k)s. Whereas those traditional plans have relatively low limits on the amount of money that can be contributed to them in a given year, deferred compensation plans typically allow the executive to defer large sums of money each year—often in the six-figure range. The money goes into the plan pretax, so income taxes are not owed on it in the year it's deferred, and will grow tax deferred until it's withdrawn—at which point, income taxes will be owed. Typically, these plans offer a number of withdrawal options, including a lump sum distribution at retirement or various installment payments (such as quarterly payments over a five-year period).

The big caveat with deferred compensation plans is that the money executives put into them may be subject to creditors' claims against the companies those executives work for. In other words, if you have a deferred compensation plan through your company and that company goes bankrupt, you could potentially lose all of the money in the plan to creditors—which might total hundreds of thousands of dollars or more. It is imperative to understand the plan design and know whether these assets could be subject to creditors' claims.

INCOME SOURCE #6: MISCELLANEOUS SOURCES

Inheritances, royalty income, and proceeds from the sale of business assets are some examples of other income sources that might be part of an investor's retirement planning.

There are other sources of income that may be available but are beyond the scope of this book. It is critical to understand the various sources and how they touch your financial situation. For example, how and when are they taxed, and what impact this will have on other areas of your wealth management plan. A wealth manager or a tax, legal, or insurance advisor can provide guidance on your specific income sources.

CHAPTER 7

Key Calculations: Finding Your "Work-Is-Optional" Number

In this chapter, we'll take a closer look at some of the calculations introduced back in chapter 1. Digging deeper here will allow you to answer two important questions about your retirement:

- *How much annual income will you need to maintain a fulfilling lifestyle in retirement?*
- *How much money do you need to make work an option, not a necessity?*

When it comes right down to it, there is one number that plays a huge role in your retirement future. I call it the Work-Is-Optional number. As the name implies, it is the amount of money you will be required to save to remove "must" from the prospect of working, and instead make work an option.

To determine your personal Work-Is-Optional number, you need to do some calculations.

ADD UP THOSE EXPENSES

The first stop on your path to your Work-Is-Optional number involves your expenses. As I pointed out in chapter 1, everyone's retirement comes with a price tag, and you've got to know yours to the best of your ability before you can confidently enter this next stage of your life.

We find that many investors who are within a few years of retiring have a good handle on their likely expenses in retirement. However, if you don't—or if you are still ten years or more from exiting the workforce—you may need some guidance.

The accompanying Budgeting Worksheet will take you through the full range of retirement expense categories so you can make estimates. Start with your core expenses, such as housing, automobiles, food, clothing, and personal items. Keep in mind that while some may decline in retirement, others will remain stable or even increase. Each situation is unique, of course, which is why the budgeting worksheet is an important tool. In the example, I have included some hypothetical numbers in various categories. If you would like to develop your own budgeting worksheet, you can download a version from our website at www.hattonconsulting.com.

Next, consider extraordinary items that you might easily overlook. These might include replacing any vehicles, unexpected home repairs or major improvements, new hobbies, or trips you have been waiting to take.

Then list your debts: mortgages, credit cards, home equity lines of credit, and any business-related debts or other obligations. It may be smart to pay off your mortgage in full before you retire—if you have the ability to do it and still have enough in your investment portfolio to meet your income shortfall in retirement. It certainly makes good sense to pay off any credit card debt and home equity lines of credit before retiring. Consumer debt tends to carry high interest charges that eat into retirement savings.

You'll also want to factor in an additional 20 percent for taxes. This is an estimate, of course, and may change based on developments in your personal financial situation as well as in tax rates between now and retirement. You should consult with your wealth manager and tax advisor to arrive at an appropriate tax withholding percentage. Where figures appear in the Budgeting Worksheet, they are for illustrative purposes only.

BUDGETING WORKSHEET

Expense Description	Monthly Expense	Yearly Expense
Primary Residence:		
Mortgage Payment (Principal and Interest Only)	$850	$10,200
Property Taxes	$300	$3,600
Home Insurance	$100	$1,200
Average Electric	$80	$960
Average Water/Sewer	$75	$900
Average Phone	$125	$1,500
Average Fuel or Gas	$40	$ 480
Trash Removal	$25	$ 300
Cable, Internet, TV	$150	$1,800
Homeowners Assoc. Dues	$200	$2,400
Misc. Maintenance	$200	$2,400
Other		
Other		
Second Residence:		
Mortgage Payment (Principal and Interest Only)		
Property Taxes		
Home Insurance		
Average Electric		
Average Water/Sewer		
Average Phone		
Average Fuel or Gas		
Trash Removal		
Cable, Internet, TV		
Homeowners Assoc. Dues		
Misc. Maintenance		
Other		
Other		
Investment Property:		
Mortgage Payment (Principal and Interest Only)	$750	$9,000
Property Taxes	$250	$3,000
Property Insurance	$75	$900
Maintenance Expense	$100	$1,200
Property Management Fee	$50	$600
Homeowners Assoc. Dues	$125	$1,500
Other		

Expense Description	Monthly Expense	Yearly Expense
Insurance:		
Health Insurance	$400	$4,800
Dental Insurance	$50	$600
Life Insurance	$125	$1,500
Long Term Care Insurance	$150	$1,800
Disability Insurance	$100	$1,200
Umbrella Insurance	$25	$300
Auto Insurance	$100	$1,200
Auto Insurance	$80	$960
Auto Insurance		
Other Insurance		
Other Insurance		
Automobiles:		
Payment 1	$225	$2,700
Payment 2	$275	$3,300
Payment 3		
Gas/Oil	$175	$2,100
Maintenance/Repairs	$50	$600
Annual Licensing	$60	$720
Car Wash	$50	$600
Other		
Other		
Groceries, Food, Leisure:		
Groceries	$500	$6,000
Meals Outside Home	$400	$4,800
Other Misc Food Expenses	$50	$600
Travel/Vacation	$500	$6,000
Entertainment	$200	$2,400
Other Credit Card	$375	$4,500
Clothing:		
Purchase	$75	$900
Cleaning/Repair	$25	$300
Other		
Gifts/Charity:		
Holiday Gifts	$150	$1,800
Birthday Gifts	$50	$600
Church	$100	$1,200
Charity	$50	$600
Other		
Other		

Expense Description	Monthly Expense	Yearly Expense
Professional Fees:		
Physician	$50	$600
Dental	$25	$300
Eye Care	$30	$360
Hair Stylist	$50	$600
Accountant	$100	$1,200
Attorney	$100	$1,200
Veterinarian	$25	$300
Other		
Miscellaneous:		
Health Club	$100	$1,200
House Cleaning	$100	$1,200
School/College		
Child Care		
Wedding		
Funeral Expenses		
Other		
Other		
Loans/Debt Payments:		
Credit Card		
Recreational Vehicle		
Home Equity Line of Credit		
Educational Loans		
Other		
Extraordinary: Auto Replacement	$252	$3,024
Total Estimated Tax (Rate Assumption 20%)	$2,166	$25,992
Gross Annual Income Need in Retirement (GAINR)	$10,833	$130,000*

* Figure rounded.

Debt Description	Amount
Mortgage Balance	$110,000
Home Equity Line of Credit	$0
Business Debt	$0
Credit Card	$0
Other	$0

FINDING YOUR SHORTFALL

Once you add up all of the expenses on the worksheet, you will arrive at your Gross Annual Income Need in Retirement (GAINR). Using the numbers in the worksheet above, let's assume your GAINR came to $130,000.

The next step: Add up all your sources of income in retirement (see chapter 7) and subtract that total from your GAINR. Let's assume your Social Security, pension, and income from real estate add up to $80,000 a year.

Then subtract the total of all income sources from your GAINR to determine your shortfall—that is, the amount of money you need to generate from your investment portfolio each year to fund your retirement needs. In this example, you would have a shortfall of $50,000 ($130,000 - $80,000).

SHORTFALL WORKSHEET

Expenses and Income Sources	Amount
Gross Annual Income Need in Retirement (GAINR)	$130,000
Less: Annual Social Security Income	($28,000)
Less: Annual Pension Income	($20,000)
Less: Rental Income from Commercial Real Estate	($32,000)
Gross Annual Income Needed From Portfolio ("Your Shortfall")	$50,000

YOUR WORK-IS-OPTIONAL NUMBER RANGE

Now that you know your shortfall, the accompanying Work-Is-Optional Worksheet will help you determine how much your portfolio will need to be worth when you retire.

Here's how it works.

1. In the worksheet, locate your Gross Annual Income Need. Let's assume that, as in the example above, the amount you will need each year is $50,000 (increasing annually by 3 percent to account for inflation).

2. Next, select how long you think your retirement will last, and how long it will be before you retire and need to start taking income from your portfolio. For example, let's assume that you will need to start taking that $50,000 annually from your portfolio when you retire ten years from now. And let's assume that your retirement will last thirty years.

Using those assumptions, you can see that your portfolio will need to be worth somewhere between $1,547,000 and $2,416,000 when you retire in ten years. The lower number in this range assumes you spend down the entire balance during your thirty-year retirement. The higher number in this range assumes you leave a balance of approximately $1,150,000 in today's dollars to pass along to your heirs.

WORK-IS-OPTIONAL WORKSHEET

Amount of Money Needed to Fund Various Levels of Income						
Gross Annual Income Need (increasing 3% annually)	Length of Retirement	Start Taking Income Now	Start Taking Income in 5 Years	Start Taking Income in 10 Years	Start Taking Income in 15 Years	Start Taking Income in 20 Years
RANGE FOR THE RETIREMENT PORTFOLIO'S STARTING VALUE* ON DAY 1 OF RETIREMENT						
$50,000	10 years	$460,000 to $839,000	$533,000 to $972,000	$618,000 to $1,127,000	$716,000 to $1,306,000	$830,000 to $1,514,000
	20 years	$839,000 to $1,409,000	$972,000 to $1,634,000	$1,127,000 to $1,894,000	$1,306,000 to $2,195,000	$1,514,000 to $2,545,000
	30 years	$1,151,000 to $1,798,000	$1,335,000 to $2,084,000	$1,547,000 to $2,416,000	$1,793,000 to $2,800,000	$2,079,000 to $3,246,000
$100,000	10 years	$919,000 to $1,677,000	$1,065,000 to $1,944,000	$1,235,000 to $2,253,000	$1,431,000 to $2,612,000	$1,659,000 to $3,028,000
	20 years	$1,677,000 to $2,818,000	$1,944,000 to $3,267,000	$2,253,000 to $3,787,000	$2,612,000 to $4,390,000	$3,028,000 to $5,089,000
	30 years	$2,302,000 to $3,595,000	$2,669,000 to $4,167,000	$3,094,000 to $4,831,000	$3,586,000 to $5,600,000	$4,157,000 to $6,492,000
$150,000	10 years	$1,378,000 to $2,515,000	$1,598,000 to $2,915,000	$1,852,000 to $3,380,000	$2,147,000 to $3,918,000	$2,489,000 to $4,542,0000
	20 years	$2,515,000 to $4,227,000	$2,915,000 to $4,900,000	$3,380,000 to $5,680,000	$3,918,000 to $6,585,000	$4,542,000 to $7,633,000
	30 years	$3,453,000 to $5,392,000	$4,003,000 to $6,250,000	$4,640,000 to $7,246,000	$5,379,000 to $8,400,000	$6,236,000 to $9,738,000
$200,000	10 years	$1,837,000 to $3,353,000	$2,130,000 to $3,887,000	$2,469,000 to $4,506,000	$2,862,000 to $5,224,000	$3,318,000 to $6,056,000
	20 years	$3,353,000 to $5,635,000	$3,887,000 to $6,533,000	$4,506,000 to $7,573,000	$5,224,000 to $8,779,000	$6,056,000 to $10,177,000
	30 years	$4,604,000 to $7,189,000	$5,337,000 to $8,334,000	$6,187,000 to $9,661,000	$7,172,000 to $11,199,000	$8,314,000 to $12,983,000

*The lower value represents the amount needed assuming an individual spends approximately all of their money during his or her life expectancy. The upper value represents the amount needed assuming an individual wishes to pass on an inheritance with approximately the same purchasing power as the lower value at the time of death. In all cases, it is assumed that the Retirement Portfolio is invested is such a way as to generate a 5% rate of return after all fees and expenses.

Please remember that past performance may not be indicative of future results. Different types of investments involve varying degrees of risk, including loss of principal, and there can be no assurance that the future performance of any specific investment or investment strategy will be profitable. Indices are unmanaged baskets of securities in which investors cannot directly invest. For illustrative purposes only.

If you are interested in calculating your specific Work-Is-Optional number, go to www.hattonconsulting.com and select the Work-Is-Optional tab.

A WEALTH OF IMPORTANT INFORMATION FOR MAKING SMART DECISIONS

By going through this process, you will know the amount of money you will need in your portfolio when you retire. Armed with that information, you can make savings and investment decisions today that will help you reach that number in the future. Ultimately, you can create a portfolio with a mix of assets (such as stocks, bonds, and cash) that have the potential to generate the annual return you need. For that, you'll need an investment policy statement that helps you stay on track. We'll turn to that now.

CHAPTER 8

Get It in Writing: A Sample Investment Policy Statement

As with any investment you make in life—in a home, a family, a child's college education—the best results are achieved by following a carefully constructed plan consistently over time.

As pointed out in chapter 2, a well-crafted investment policy statement provides context for making important financial decisions and prescribes a prudent investment process to achieve long-term financial and other wealth management goals.

Here is a closer look at the investment policy statement—what it does, the benefits it confers, and examples of information contained in a well-crafted IPS.

THE ROLE OF THE IPS

The investment policy statement is designed to accomplish several things:

1. **Set objectives.** The IPS declares your retirement goals and expectations, both financial and personal (including retirement income needs and sources of income).

2. **Define investment management policy.** The IPS identifies the asset classes in which you will invest and specifies the proportion that each class is to have in your portfolio. It sets forth the expected portfolio investment returns, the specific investments to be used, rebalancing guidelines, and fees.

3. **Establish management procedures.** The IPS lists the criteria for selecting the investments in your portfolio, monitoring and evaluating investment performance and fees, and deciding when changes will be made. It says who will be responsible for executing each of the components of the policy.

4. **Determine communication protocols.** The IPS helps all the people involved in the management of the portfolio—including each of your professional advisors—understand how to communicate and interact with each other on your behalf.

THE BENEFITS OF USING AN IPS

Articulating all this in an investment plan has important benefits:

1. It gives you a disciplined, systematic approach to making investment-related decisions. A well-conceived plan helps assure that rational analysis is the basis for your investment decisions, making you less likely to act on emotional responses to short-term or one-time events. When you maintain a disciplined approach, you're less liable to sell investments at the wrong time during periods of market stress. Likewise, it helps you stick to your plan during strong markets, when there can be significant temptation to load up on the hottest performing asset classes.

2. It encourages effective communication. Because it spells out your goals and the strategy that will be used to pursue them, the IPS minimizes any misunderstandings that may arise. All parties involved in managing your wealth can use the IPS to give themselves a full understanding of their roles, duties, and functions. In short, it puts everyone on the same page and makes expectations clear.

3. It gives you and your advisor(s) a reliable reference point for accurate reviews of your situation as it develops over time. Such evaluations may indicate that corresponding changes to your investment plan are called for.

To put it another way: An investment policy statement spells out, in plain language, your investing "dos" and "don'ts"—helping everyone involved in the management of your wealth use their heads and not their hearts when making decisions and recommendations.

A SAMPLE IPS

To see how an IPS can help you make smart and rational choices instead of emotional decisions from the gut, consider the information that goes into it. Here's a sample IPS that reflects the type of document we would prepare at Hatton Consulting. Your IPS may include different specifics, of course, but will generally follow this approach.

SECTION ONE: CLIENT PROFILE

Information obtained during the discovery meeting, described in chapter 1, is organized in this first section.

Summary
- Robert A. Smith, born January 1, 1949, and Mary L. Smith, born March 1, 1949.
- In our discovery meeting on February 15, 2014, you shared with us many important insights into your financial situation, the challenges you face, and the goals you seek to accomplish. The summary below reflects our understanding of these issues in several key areas.

I. Financial Values

You described the importance of money to you as follows:
A. Remain independent throughout retirement and not be a burden to our kids as we age.
B. Provide for our retirement lifestyle without financial worry.

II. Goals

You described your top personal and financial goals as follows:

A. Personal
1. Travel internationally (twice each year).
2. Spend time with children and grandchildren.

B. Financial
1. Generate an inflation adjusted income of $51,800 annually in retirement (3% inflation adjustment).

2. Purchase cabin (20% likelihood). Budget $150,000.
3. Build investment strategies to minimize federal and state tax liabilities.
4. Evaluate trust document, amend if necessary. Consider alternate successor trustee.
5. Budget $5,000 annually for giving to church/charitable organizations.
6. Contribute to grandchildren's education accounts. Amount to be determined.
7. Review asset protection strategies.
8. Review need and alternative uses for life insurance cash values.

III. Relationships

A. You described your most important relationships as follows:
   1. Robert Smith Jr. (33), son. Lives in Phoenix and is an accountant. Married to Barb (32). There are two children.
   2. Kathy Smith-Brown (31), daughter. Lives in Phoenix and is an RN. Married to Mike (32). There are two children.
   3. The grandchildren: Rick, Jack, Ellie, and Anna.
   4. Our church.
   5. Our pet dog, Cosmo.

B. You identified your Executor/Personal Representative and/or Successor Trustees:
   1. Robert Smith Jr. Executor/Personal Representative.
   2. Kathy Smith-Brown. Successor Trustee.

IV. Assets

You identified these major assets:

A. Income Sources
   1. Robert's salary, $200,000. Robert's bonus, $100,000.
   2. Mary's salary, $80,000.
   3. Social Security benefit: Bob @ 66, $2,500/mo.; at 70, $3,300/mo.
   4. Social Security benefit: Mary @ 66, $1,800/mo.; at 70, $2,376/mo.
   5. Pension benefit: Mary @ 66 $800/mo. 50% survivor ($1,000/mo. single life).
   6. Rental income, currently receiving $1,000/month net.

B. Financial Assets
   1. Smith Revocable Trust (non-qualified): $1,000,000.
   2. Robert Smith IRA (qualified): $300,000.
   3. Mary Smith IRA (qualified): $375,000.
   4. Robert Smith Annuity (qualified): $50,000.
   5. Robert Smith 401(k) (qualified): $500,000.
   6. Mary Smith 401(k) (qualified): $150,000.
   7. Checking (non-qualified): $15,000.
   8. Savings (non-qualified): $200,000.

   Sub-Total Non-Qualified Assets: $1,215,000.
   Sub-Total Qualified Assets: $1,375,000.
   Total Financial Assets: $2,590,000.

C. Non-Financial Assets or Financial Assets Held in Custody by Others
   1. Personal Property: $450,000.
   2. Future inheritance (excluded from net worth total): $200,000.

Total non-financial assets (excluding financial assets held in custody by others): $450,000.

D. Real Estate Assets
   1. Residence: $850,000 market value, $0 mortgage balance, $850,000 equity value.
   2. Rental: $200,000 market value, $0 mortgage balance, $200,000 equity value.

Total Real Estate Equity: $1,050,000

E. Insurance Assets
   1. MetLife Universal Life policy: Insured life, Robert. $250,000 benefit, $125,000 cash value. Beneficiary is Mary.
   2. MetLife Universal Life policy: Insured life, Mary. $250,000 benefit, $90,000 cash value. Beneficiary is Robert.

Life Insurance Total Cash Value: $215,000

F. Summary of Combined Net Worth

SUMMARY OF COMBINED NET WORTH

Description	Amount
Qualified Investment Portfolio assets:	$1,375,000
Non-Qualified Investment Portfolio assets:	$1,215,000
Aggregate Investment Portfolio:	**$2,590,000**
Personal Property:	$450,000 ·
Total Real Estate Equity:	$1,050,000
Life Insurance Total Cash Value:	$215,000
Estimated Net Worth:	**$4,305,000**
Estimated net effective tax bracket:	20%

V. Advisors

You stated that you are currently working with or have worked with the following professional advisor(s):

A. Tax Preparer/CPA: Bob Adams, (212) 555-4321; bob@__.com
B. Estate/Trust Attorney: Sherry Williams, (312) 555-7654; sherry@___.biz
C. Personal Insurance Advisor: Joe Wilson, (213) 555-7890; joe@_____.net

VI. Process

You described your preferred process for working with your wealth manager as follows:

A. Meet twice annually with financial advisor.
B. Meet with financial advisor and tax advisor in a joint meeting once per year.

C. Meet with estate planning attorney as needed or at least once
every four years.

VII. Interests/Hobbies

You described the following personal interests as being most important to you:

A. Family
B. Travel
C. Fitness
D. Reading

SECTION TWO: THE INVESTMENT PLAN

The investment plan section consists of two parts:

I. An analysis of your current situation
II. Hatton Consulting's recommendations for achieving your
financial goals

I. Current Situation

Income, Savings, and Expenses Analysis (in present value terms)
Analysis of Five-Year Cash Flow

Annual Income:

INVESTMENT PLAN ANALYSIS

Annual Income	Bob	Mary
Robert's salary/Mary's salary	$200,000 (Years: 1)	$80,000 (Years: 1)
Robert's bonus/Mary's bonus	$100,000 (Years: 1)	$0 (Years: 1)
Social Security	$30,000 (Years: 4)	$21,600 (Years: 4)
Pension	$0 (Years: 5)	$9,600 (Years: 5)
Rental income	$12,000 (Years: 5)	$0 (Years: 5)
Five-Year Total	$480,000	$204,800
Aggregate Total	$684,000	

Estimated Savings	Account Saved to	From Year	To Year
$22,880	Bob 401(k)	2014	2015
$22,440	Mary 401(k)	2014	2015
$100,000	Trust	2014	2015

Regular Expenses	
Estimated Annual Living Expenses	$100,000 net of income taxes; $125,000 including income taxes
Five-Year Total	$500,000 net of income taxes; $625,000 including income taxes

Extraordinary Expenses	
Housing expenses	$0
Vacation expenses	$0
Automobile expenses	$40,000 new car
College expenses	$0
Other	$0

Investment Portfolio: Current Asset Allocation Analysis

As seen in the Current Asset Allocation pie chart, currently your Investment Portfolio's broad asset allocation is 62 percent equity securities, 20 percent fixed-income securities and cash, and 18 percent alternative securities.

CURRENT ASSET ALLOCATION

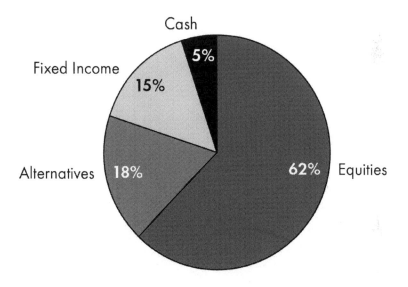

II. Recommendations

We used the following steps to develop our recommended asset allocation for your investment portfolio(s):

1. Assess your goals and circumstances.
2. Determine your Target Rate of Return (minimum investment return needed to reach your goals and objectives).
3. Determine your Asset Allocation/Risk Tolerance (select appropriate mix of equity and fixed income investments expected to generate your Target Rate of Return over the long term with the least amount of risk).

RECOMMENDED ASSET ALLOCATION

Description	Amount
Annual income you want for living expenses (excluding taxes)	$100,000
Total income needed including taxes, based on a 20% effective tax rate	$125,000
Less: Annual Social Security Income, before taxes	($51,600)
Less: Annual Pension Income, before taxes	($9,600)
Less: Rental Income, before taxes	($12,000)
Estimated annual income needed from the total portfolio	**$51,800**
Total Current Portfolio Value	$2,590,000
Target rate of return (TRR) before inflation	2.0%
Estimated inflation rate	3.0%
TRR with inflation adjustment	**5.0%**

Based on our analysis to determine the estimated return needed to meet your income and investment goals, both with and without inflation, we recommend the following asset allocation.

Estimated return needed from all investments to meet income/investment goals, without inflation: 2%
Estimated return needed from all investments to meet income/investment goals, with inflation: 5%

SPECIFIC PORTFOLIO MIX

Account(s)	Trust	Robert IRA	Mary IRA	Annuity	Blended
Equity Allocation	40%	40%	40%	40%	40%
Fixed Income Allocation	60%	60%	60%	60%	60%
ANNUALIZED RETURN The projected annualized nominal return for the portfolio.	5.4%	5.4%	5.4%	5.4%	5.4%
LIKELY RANGE OF RETURNS There is a 96% chance that any one year's nominal return will fall within this range.	18.6% to -7.8%	18.6% to -7.8%	18.6% to -7.8%	18.6% to -7.8%	18.6% to -7.8%
LARGE DECLINE SCENARIO There is a 2% chance that any one year's nominal return will be as bad as or worse than this.	-7.8%	-7.8%	-7.8%	-7.8%	-7.8%

Account Name & Objective: Trust: Current Income with Some Capital Appreciation.
Allocated 40% to equities, 60% to fixed-income.

TRUST ALLOCATION

Broad Asset Class	Target Allocation	Buy when Target Below	Sell when Target Above	Investment Vehicle
Cash & Equivalents	5%	3.75%	6.25%	Money Market
Inflation-Protected Securities	5.5%	4.125%	6.875%	VTAPX
High-Quality Fixed Income (Ultra Short Term)	16.5%	12.375%	20.625%	DFIHX
High-Quality Fixed Income (Short Term)	16.5%	12.375%	20.625%	VFSUX
High-Quality Fixed Income (Intermediate Term)	16.5%	12.375%	20.625%	VFIDX
U.S. Core Equity	20%	15%	25%	DFQTX
U.S. Real Estate (REIT)	4%	3%	5%	DFREX
International Core Equity	12.8%	9.6%	16%	DFIEX
Emerging Markets Core Equity	3.2%	2.4%	4%	DFCEX
TOTAL	100%			

TRUST ALLOCATION

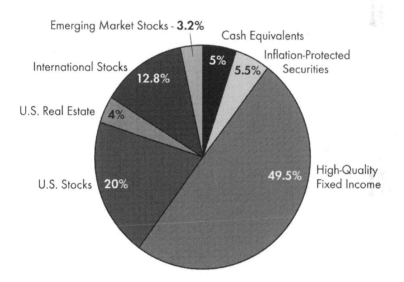

Account Name & Objective: Robert IRA: Current Income with Some Capital Appreciation.

Allocated 40% to equities, 60% to fixed-income.

ROBERT IRA ALLOCATION

Broad Asset Class	Target Allocation	Buy when Target Below	Sell when Target Above	Investment Vehicle
Inflation Protected Securities	6%	4.5%	7.5%	VTAPX
High Quality Fixed Income (Ultra Short Term)	18%	13.5%	22.5%	DFIHX
High Quality Fixed Income (Short Term)	18%	13.5%	22.5%	VFSUX
High Quality Fixed Income (Intermediate Term)	18%	13.5%	22.5%	VFIDX
U.S. Core Equity	20%	15%	25%	DFQTX
U.S. Real Estate (REIT)	4%	3%	5%	DFREX
International Core Equity	12.8%	9.6%	16%	DFIEX
Emerging Markets Core Equity	3.2%	2.4%	4%	DFCEX
TOTAL	100%			

ROBERT IRA ALLOCATION

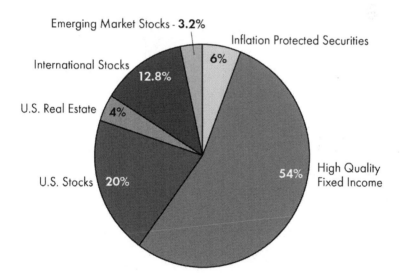

Account Name & Objective: Mary IRA: Current Income with Some Capital Appreciation.
Allocated 40% to equities, 60% to fixed-income.

MARY IRA ALLOCATION

Broad Asset Class	Target Allocation	Buy when Target Below	Sell when Target Above	Investment Vehicle
Inflation Protected Securities	6%	4.5%	7.5%	VTAPX
High Quality Fixed Income (Ultra Short Term)	18%	13.5%	22.5%	DFIHX
High Quality Fixed Income (Short Term)	18%	13.5%	22.5%	VFSUX
High Quality Fixed Income (Intermediate Term)	18%	13.5%	22.5%	VFIDX
U.S. Core Equity	20%	15%	25%	DFQTX
U.S. Real Estate (REIT)	4%	3%	5%	DFREX
International Core Equity	12.8%	9.6%	16%	DFIEX
Emerging Markets Core Equity	3.2%	2.4%	4%	DFCEX
TOTAL	100%			

MARY IRA ALLOCATION

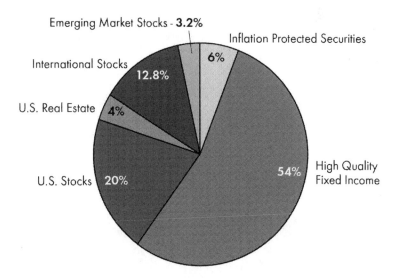

Account Name & Objective: Annuity: Current Income with Some Capital Appreciation.
Allocated 40% to equities, 60% to fixed-income.

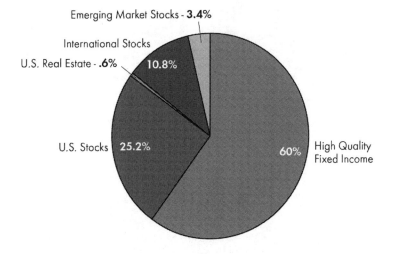

ANNUITY ALLOCATION

Broad Asset Class	Target Allocation	Buy when Target Below	Sell when Target Above	Investment Vehicle
High Quality Fixed Income	60%	45%	75%	DFAPX
Global Equity	40%	30%	50%	DGEIX
TOTAL	100%			

Emerging Market Stocks - **3.4%**

International Stocks

U.S. Real Estate - **.6%**   10.8%

U.S. Stocks **25.2%**   60%   High Quality Fixed Income

REBALANCING GUIDELINES

We will consider rebalancing the portfolio back to the target allocation when the overall allocation or sub-asset classes deviate by plus or minus 25 percent from the initial allocation. For example, if a particular asset class has a target allocation of 10 percent, rebalancing will be considered if that asset class falls to 7.5 percent or rises to 12.5 percent.

Rebalancing is not automatic if an asset class reaches an upper or lower limit. When contemplating rebalancing, one consideration is the potential tax impact of the rebalancing itself. If you are holding positions with substantial unrealized gains, it may be advantageous to use cash inflows or outflows to rebalance the portfolio. We will deploy cash inflows/outflows in such a way as to bring the portfolio back to the target allocation. In the absence of inflows/outflows, transactions may be made only after all ramifications have been considered.

The accompanying table, Rebalancing Guidelines, shows the current amount of unrealized gains and losses, as well as any carry-forward loss from your existing account(s) outside Hatton Consulting, Inc. To create your optimal portfolio using the target asset allocations recommended above, we may (to the extent possible) offset unrealized gains with unrealized and/or carry-forward losses in order to build the portfolio in the most tax-efficient way.

UNREALIZED GAIN/LOSS

Account(s)	Unrealized Gain/Loss	Realized Gain/Loss	Carry-Forward Loss
Smith Revocable Trust	$15,000	$0	$0
TOTAL	**$15,000**	**$0**	**$0**

SECTION THREE: INVESTMENT MANAGEMENT FEES

There are three levels of fees associated with the wealth management process:

Level 1: Asset management fees (for managing mutual funds, separate accounts, etc.)

Level 2: Custodial/Transaction fees (for buying and selling securities)

Level 3: Advisory fees (for managing the wealth management process)

Level 1: Asset Management Fees

The accompanying table, Asset Management Fees, summarizes fees typically charged by mutual fund companies and separate-account managers of the individual investment options selected for your account(s)—which is expressed by the *expense ratio*—and each option's turnover ratio. These are compared to the median expense and turnover ratios for the asset classes recommended for your portfolio. These ratios are important when considering the costs of investing. In general, lower ratios indicate more cost-effective and tax-efficient investment options.

ASSET MANAGEMENT FEES

Asset Class	Benchmark	Median Expense Ratio %	Median Turnover Ratio %	Selected Fund Name	Fund Symbol	Fund Expense Ratio %	Fund Turnover Ratio %
US STOCKS							
U.S. Core Equity	Russell 3000	1.08	41	DFA US Core Equity 2	DFQTX	0.22	5
U.S. Real Estate (REIT)	Dow Jones US Select REIT	1.22	44	DFA Real Estate Securities	DFREX	0.18	0
INTERNATIONAL STOCKS							
International Core Equity	MSCI World ex USA	1.26	42	DFA International Core Equity	DFIEX	0.40	5
Emerging Markets Core Equity	MSCI Emerging	1.49	55	DFA Emerging Markets Core Equity	DFCEX	0.68	1
BALANCED FUNDS							
Global Equity	MSCI World ND	1.36	42	DFA Global Equity	DGEIX	0.33	0
FIXED INCOME							
Money Market	BofA Merrill Lynch 6 mo. US Treas. Bill	0.00	0	Cash / Equivalent	Money Market	0.00	N/A
Inflation Protected Securities	Barclays U.S. Treasury TIPS	0.67	55	Vanguard Short-Term Infl-Prot Sec Idx Adm	VTAPX	0.10	0
High Quality Fixed Income (Ultra Short Term)	BofA Merrill Lynch 1 yr. US Treas. Note	0.55	65	DFA One-Year Fixed-Income	DFIHX	0.17	77
High Quality Fixed Income (Short Term)	Barclays Gov't/ Credit 1-5 yr.	0.75	73	Vanguard Short-Term Investment-Grade Adm	VFSUX	0.10	80
High Quality Fixed Income (Intermediate Term)	Barclays Gov't/ Credit 5-10 yr.	0.80	141	Vanguard Interm-Term Investment-Grde Adm	VFIDX	0.10	62
High Quality Fixed Income	Barclays U.S. Aggregate Bond	0.80	141	DFA Investment Grade	DFAPX	0.22	0

Source: Morningstar via Fiduciary Analytics (www.fi360.com), September 30, 2013

Level 2: Custodial/Transactions Fees

Transaction fees for trading stocks, bonds, and mutual funds are charged by the custodian and are subject to change. These fees are generally quite low. For example, a typical stock trade might cost approximately $10 to $20. None of these fees are received by Hatton Consulting, Inc.

Level 3: Advisory Fees

Here are some examples of advisory fees that clients of a wealth manager might pay for creating and managing their personal wealth management plans.

ADVISORY FEES

Account Value	Fee Range
$0 to $1,000,000	0.5% to 1% of portfolio assets
$1,000,001 to $2,000,000	0.4% to 0.6% of portfolio assets
$2,000,001 to $5,000,000	0.25% to 0.4% of portfolio assets
$5,000,001 to $20,000,000	0.10% to 0.25% of portfolio assets
$20,000,001 and ABOVE	0.05 to 0.10% of portfolio assets

Total Estimated Annual Fees, as a Percentage of Assets	
Level 1: Asset Management Fees:	0.20%
Level 2: Custodial/Transaction Fees:	0.03%
Level 3: Advisory Fees:	0.83%
TOTAL FEES:	1.06%

SECTION FOUR: INVESTMENT SELECTION CRITERIA

For an investment to be used in a portfolio, it must score well based on the following eleven criteria, which have been created by fi360. The fi360 Fiduciary Score® is a peer percentile ranking of an investment against a set of quantitative due-diligence criteria selected to reflect prudent fiduciary management.

fi360 Fiduciary Score® Criteria

1. Inception Date: The investment must have at least a three-year track history.
2. Manager Tenure: The most-senior investment manager must have at least a two-year track history.
3. Assets: The investment must have at least $75 million (in total across all share classes for funds/ETFs) under management.
4. Composition: The investment's allocation to its primary asset class should be greater than or equal to 80%.
5. Style: The investment's current style box should match the peer group's.
6. Prospectus Net Expense Ratio: The investment must place in the top 75% of its peer group.
7. Alpha: The investment must place in the top 50% of its peer group.
8. Sharpe Ratio: The investment must place in the top 50% of its peer group.
9. 1-Year Return: The investment must place in the top 50% of its peer group.
10. 3-Year Return: The investment must place in the top 50% of its peer group.
11. 5-Year Return: The investment must place in the top 50% of its peer group.

SECTION FIVE: MONITORING

Annually, we will review the goals and objectives of the investment policy statement with the client to ensure they are relevant and up-to-date. We will compare actual investment results to the stated investment objectives in the IPS to track overall progress. Quarterly, we will send performance reports to the client that document after-fee performance for multiple time periods.

Additionally, we will monitor investment vehicles to verify the manager's performance versus criteria identified in Section Four of this IPS. The client acknowledges that fluctuating rates of returns associated with the stock market may deviate from the investment objectives, particularly in short time periods. Therefore, we will evaluate progress of investment managers and portfolio returns from a long-term perspective.

ADDRESSING ADVANCED CONCERNS

Once your investments are positioned appropriately and you have an IPS to keep you on track, it is time to start addressing your noninvestment financial concerns. In the next chapter, we'll take a closer look at the first component of the advanced planning process: tax planning.

CHAPTER 9

Advanced Planning Strategy #1: Tax Planning

Investment planning is only one part of the consultative wealth management process. As I pointed out in earlier chapters, in order for affluent investors to coordinate their financial lives and manage their wealth with the whole picture in mind, they must also focus on more advanced issues that can impact their financial security and peace of mind.

Tax planning is the foundation for the other advanced strategies central to excellent wealth management. The reason is obvious: Taxes impact virtually everyone; there's a reason that Ben Franklin said, "Nothing can be said to be certain, except death and taxes." That's especially true for investors and families with significant wealth. Studies have confirmed that minimizing income tax and capital gains taxes is of prime concern to most affluent investors.

This chapter explores tax planning concepts and offers strategies that can help to mitigate the impact that taxes have on your financial health and well-being. It also speaks to one of the biggest concerns that many of our clients face: generating income from investments to pay for retirement expenses.

A few caveats: The tax rates cited in this chapter were accurate as of the writing of this book. However, as you're well aware, changes to tax laws occur frequently. It's important to revisit the rules regularly to ensure that you are up-to-date on the latest developments and can plan accordingly. What's more, strategies mentioned in this chapter may not be appropriate for or benefit all investors. Each person's tax situation is unique and has to be taken into account before engaging in any particular strategy. Work with your tax advisor before implementing any strategy.

TAXES: AN OVERVIEW

The origins of taxes as we know them today can be traced to 1862 when, to help finance the Civil War, Congress enacted the nation's first income tax law. Later, in 1913, the Sixteenth Amendment to the Constitution made income tax a permanent fixture.

Today, the most common types of taxes investors face include the following:

Ordinary Income Taxes. Examples of ordinary income include wages, interest, and rent from investment-related properties. Many investments—including savings accounts, certificates of deposit, money market accounts, annuities, bonds, and some preferred stock—can generate ordinary income. At the time of this writing, ordinary income is taxed at the tax rates shown in the accompanying table, 2014 Tax Brackets.

2014 TAX BRACKETS

Tax rate	Single filers	Married filing jointly or qualifying widow/widower	Married filing separately	Head of household
10%	Up to $9,075	Up to $18,150	Up to $9,075	Up to $12,950
15%	$9,076 to $36,900	$18,151 to $73,800	$9,076 to $36,900	$12,951 to $49,400
25%	$36,901 to $89,350	$73,801 to $148,850	$36,901 to $74,425	$49,401 to $127,550
28%	$89,351 to $186,350	$148,851 to $226,850	$74,426 to $113,425	$127,551 to $206,600
33%	$186,351 to $405,100	$226,851 to $405,100	$113,426 to $202,550	$206,601 to $405,100
35%	$405,101 to $406,750	$405,101 to $457,600	$202,551 to $228,800	$405,101 to $432,200
39.6%	$406,751 or more	$457,601 or more	$228,801 or more	$432,201 or more

Capital Gains Taxes. This tax is triggered when you sell an investment at a higher price than you paid for it. The amount of tax you pay depends on several factors—such as how long you have owned the investment and your overall taxable income. For example:

1. Short-term capital gains are gains on assets owned for one year or less. They are taxed at the ordinary income tax rates shown above.

2. Long-term capital gains are gains on assets owned for at least one year plus one day. They are taxed based on your overall income tax bracket. For example, your long-term capital gains tax rate is

- 0 percent if you are in the 10 or 15 percent marginal income tax brackets,
- 15 percent if you are in the 25, 28, 33, or 35 percent marginal income tax brackets, and
- 20 percent if you are in the 39.6 percent marginal income tax bracket.

High-income earners also pay an additional investment income tax of 3.8 percent. This tax applies to net investment income if your modified taxable income is over $125,000 if you're married filing separately, $200,000 if you file single or as a head of household, or $250,000 if you're married filing jointly or a qualifying widow(er) with a dependent child.

3. Qualified dividends are those from shares in domestic corporations and qualified foreign corporations that you have held for at least a specified minimum period of time.

- Your qualified dividends tax rate is 0 percent if you are in the 10 or 15 percent marginal income tax bracket.
- A top rate of 15 percent applies to qualified dividends for single filers with taxable income from $36,901 up to $406,750 (from $73,801 up to $457,600 for married filing jointly). Qualified dividend income over that threshold is taxed at a rate of 20 percent.
- To be considered qualified, the shares also have to un-hedged—with no puts, calls, or short sales on the shares during the holding period.

TOP STRATEGIES FOR MINIMIZING TAXES

There are many ways to structure and manage an investment portfolio that will help to minimize the impact of taxes on it. Here are some of the most effective strategies we use at Hatton Consulting:

1. Harvest tax losses. When the value of an investment you own in a taxable account declines below the price you paid for it, you can choose to sell it at a loss. Why might you book that loss instead of holding on and hoping the investment will rebound? Because you can later use that loss to offset a gain from another investment that comes with a tax liability, thereby reducing your overall tax bill. This is called tax loss harvesting.

To see how tax loss harvesting can work, consider this example. Say you bought $100,000 of a mutual fund in your taxable account a year and a half ago. Today, however, your investment is worth just $90,000. If you sell that fund, you will realize (or book) a capital loss of $10,000. You can then use that $10,000 loss to offset up to $10,000 in realized capital gains elsewhere in your portfolio—which might occur if you sell another fund at a profit, or if funds you own distribute capital gains. If you don't have any current capital gains to offset, you can use those losses to offset as much as $3,000 in ordinary income per year, with the remaining losses carried forward to future years.

When tax loss harvesting, look to sell investments that don't fit your strategy anymore or that you can replace with other investments that are similar to the one you're selling. That said, don't violate the "wash sale" rule. According to the IRS, a wash sale occurs when you sell a security at a loss and within thirty days before or after the sale, you do the following:

- buy a substantially identical security to the one you sold at a loss
- acquire a substantially identical security in a fully taxable trade
- acquire a contract or option to buy a substantially identical security
- acquire a substantially identical security for your IRA or Roth IRA

If you violate the wash sale rule, the IRS will not allow you to take the tax deduction.

2. Shelter income from federal and state taxes. Investors in higher income tax brackets may want to consider including municipal bonds (and muni bond funds) as part of their fixed income holdings. These bonds are issued by governments, hospitals, utility companies, and other types of public entities to fund projects such as new roads, schools, and hospitals. The income generated by tax-free municipal bonds (and municipal bond funds) is sheltered from federal income taxes (and often from state and local taxes as well).

3. Use asset location strategies. Asset location strategies focus on where each type of investment in a portfolio should be placed—either a taxable account or a tax-deferred account—in order to minimize taxes and achieve the best possible after-tax return. The ideal location for each asset depends on a variety of factors such as current and future tax rates, your current and future income tax bracket, and the types of investments you own. In general, equity investments such as stock funds, which typically don't produce substantial amounts of ordinary income, are best placed in taxable accounts. Bond funds, which do generate regular income that is taxed at relatively high ordinary income tax rates, are best located in tax-deferred accounts such as IRAs (or tax-free accounts such as Roth IRAs, 529 education accounts, or health savings accounts, or HSAs). That said, no two investors are alike, and appropriate asset location strategies can be different for each investor. You will want to consult your tax advisor before making these decisions.

4. Use mutual funds with low turnover ratios. Some mutual funds help to minimize taxes by keeping their turnover rates extremely low. Turnover refers to the amount of trading that a mutual fund manager does inside of a portfolio. Managers who make a lot of trades tend to generate higher taxes, because many of those trades generate capital gains that are passed along to fund shareholders. In stark contrast, some mutual funds trade very little—their turnover rates are much lower than typical funds (see the Turnover Rates table for some examples of how low-turnover asset class funds stack up to their higher-turnover peers).

TURNOVER RATES
Asset Class Funds vs. Peer Group Median Mutual Funds

Asset Class Fund	Turnover Rate	Peer Group	Turnover Rate
DFA U.S. Core Equity II	3%	Large Blend (median fund)	38%
DFA Real Estate Securities Portfolio	1%	Real Estate (median fund)	59%
DFA Emerging Markets Core Equity Portfolio	1%	Diversified Emerging Markets (median fund)	55%

Source: Fiduciary Analytics, June 30, 2014

5. Convert to a Roth IRA when you retire. If you have a traditional IRA, it can make sense in certain circumstances to convert part of that IRA to a Roth IRA once you retire. One of the best reasons to do a partial conversion, from a tax standpoint, is that you will end up with less money in your traditional IRA than you would have otherwise. When it comes time to start taking your required minimum distribution (RMD) from your traditional IRA at age 70 ½, that lower account balance will mean you'll be required to withdraw a smaller amount of money from it each year. And, as noted above, since RMDs are taxed at ordinary income tax rates, that adds up to potentially significant tax savings.

It's best to consider this strategy if you are squarely in a relatively low effective tax bracket upon your retirement. Otherwise, the conversion could bump you up into a higher tax bracket in the year you make the conversion.

6. Use charitable donations to reduce tax liability. It's well known that donating to charity reduces your taxable income. But there are savvy ways to do it that will help take a bigger chunk out of your tax bill every April.

One example: Retirees aged 70 ½ or older can donate up to $100,000 per year tax-free from their IRA. If those assets are transferred directly from the IRA to a charity, the transfer is not considered to be part of taxable income for that year.

Another tax-savvy approach is to donate highly appreciated assets—stocks, bonds, funds, and certain other kinds of assets—that have risen significantly in value over time. By donating assets with unrealized long-term capital gains directly to a charity instead of selling them first and then donating the proceeds, no capital gains taxes are generated. The more the assets have appreciated, the greater the tax savings. What's more, a tax deduction can be taken for the full fair market value of the donated securities (up to 50 percent of the donor's adjusted gross income for qualified charities, with any excess deduction carried forward for up to five subsequent tax years).

7. Use Health Savings Accounts. HSAs are components of high-deductible HSA-compatible health insurance plans. If you have such a plan, you can open an HSA and contribute pretax money to it—thereby reducing your adjusted gross income for tax purposes. Not only are contributions tax free, so are the earnings you generate from interest and investments owned in the HSA and the distributions you take from it to pay for qualified medical expenses. These benefits can be especially appealing to retirees. Instead of tapping a 401(k) or IRA to pay for medical expenses in retirement—and paying ordinary income tax rates on the withdrawals—retirees can pull money tax-free from their HSAs. Also, there are no income limits or phaseouts for the tax deductions, which can make HSAs attractive to high earners who might have too much income to be eligible for other deductions. One note: You can't contribute to an HSA if you are already on Medicare, but you can continue to tap an HSA that you set up before enrolling.

8. Consider making a nondeductible contribution to your IRA. Although you are unable to take an immediate deduction for the contribution to the account, the earnings in the account grow tax deferred.

TAX STRATEGIES FOR WITHDRAWING RETIREMENT INCOME

When it comes time in retirement to tap into the nest egg you have built, it makes sense to do so in the most tax-advantaged ways possible. For most investors, there is a clear order to follow:

1. Tap taxable accounts first. The reason to look to taxable accounts first is that you'll likely pay *capital gains* or *qualified-dividend* tax rates on the securities you'll sell from these accounts to generate income. Those rates may be lower than the *ordinary income* tax rate you'll pay by selling securities held in tax-deferred accounts such as 401(k)s or traditional IRAs. If you've been automatically reinvesting the dividends, interest, and capital gains generated in your taxable accounts,, once you're retired, it may be prudent to turn off that reinvestment process and take the distributions in cash to help cover your income needs.

In addition, by holding off on tapping assets in your retirement accounts, you give those assets more time to grow tax-deferred. And as we've seen, there are ways to help minimize the capital gains taxes you pay on withdrawals from taxable accounts, such as tax-loss harvesting.

2. Next, tap tax-deferred accounts such as IRAs. Once you have used up your taxable accounts, it's time to take income from tax-deferred accounts. You will pay ordinary income tax rates on these withdrawals. Also, you may be aware that tax-deferred accounts such as IRAs and 401(k)s are subject to required minimum distributions— which, as the term suggests, are minimum amounts of money the IRS requires you to withdraw from your accounts each year. When you reach age 70½—regardless of whether you have retired or not—you must start taking these required withdrawals annually. (Exceptions to this rule can apply. For example, if you are still working and participating in an employer-sponsored retirement plan, required minimum distributions for that account can be delayed until full retirement.) The money you withdraw generally will be taxed at ordinary income tax rates.

3. Finally, tap tax-free accounts such as Roth IRAs. As with a traditional IRA, the earnings on a Roth IRA grow tax-deferred over time. But unlike a traditional IRA, if you are 59½ and have owned a Roth IRA for at least five years, withdrawals from your Roth are tax free. Another reason to hold off on tapping a Roth is that—unlike traditional IRAs—you aren't required to take minimum distributions from a Roth. If you end up not needing the money in your Roth, you can leave it to your heirs tax free.

ONE PIECE OF THE PUZZLE

Strategies like these set the stage for looking at other advanced-planning issues that you face now, or are likely to face in the future. Tax planning can go long way to enhancing your wealth, but it is not sufficient on its own. Further planning must be brought to bear on your situation in order to maximize your chances of achieving your goals. The next chapter will explore one of the most important and most misunderstood areas of consultative wealth-management planning: estate planning.

CHAPTER 10

Advanced Planning Strategy #2: Estate Planning

One of the most important but overlooked concerns that investors with wealth face today is estate planning.

It's no surprise that many investors don't tackle estate planning and wealth transfer head-on. The topic requires us to confront issues that can be uncomfortable to think about—such as health problems and death. It's tempting to push these aside and deal with them later on down the road.

However, delaying decisions about estate planning can have calamitous consequences. A lack of planning can result in your assets being hung up in probate, or having your assets go to people who you'd rather not see possess them, or putting a burden on your family members to make decisions about your health and wealth that they may not feel comfortable making. Lack of planning also can result in potential estate tax liability. Your interests and the interests of your family are poorly served if you ignore estate planning.

This chapter will offer questions and issues to consider as you look to begin formulating an effective wealth transfer strategy. It also will offer information about an important aspect of estate planning: selecting an appropriate trustee. It will help you create a foundation for your estate planning that can be built upon through coordinated efforts with your financial, legal, and tax advisors. A detailed analysis of specific types of trusts and estate planning vehicles is beyond the scope of this chapter. Your advisors can discuss the answers to these questions (along with a list of your financial assets) and then develop a legal structure using specific strategies that are informed by your foundation work and that are designed around the goals you identify.

BENEFITS OF ESTATE PLANNING

First, let's get clear on some important terms. Estate planning involves decisions about the management and disposition of your estate when you are no longer able to manage your own affairs due to incapacitation or death. Such planning should be done by virtually all investors and families, regardless of their level of affluence. However, it becomes of paramount importance for the wealthy, who risk losing more if they do not put their financial houses in order.

Your estate is everything you own, minus your mortgages and other debts. It most likely includes real property such as your home, your investments (stocks, bonds, annuities, mutual funds, cash, etc.) in taxable and retirement accounts, life insurance policies, and personal property such as jewelry, furniture, automobiles, appliances, and collectibles.

Estate planning offers eight substantial benefits:

1. It provides guidance and financial security for your loved ones (spouse, children, grandchildren, others) if you die or are unable to make decisions for yourself.
2. It helps ensure that the provisions of the estate plan are executed properly and in accordance with your goals.
3. It safeguards wealth for generations to come.

4. It ensures that your estate is distributed efficiently, with few legal headaches.

5. It minimizes expenses and taxes.

6. It minimizes potential issues with beneficiaries regarding the settling of your estate.

7. It ensures cash is available to settle your final affairs.

8. It helps to maintain family harmony and values across the generations.

A FRAMEWORK FOR MAKING INTELLIGENT ESTATE PLANNING DECISIONS

The first step in conducting effective estate planning is to ask yourself a series of questions about various challenging scenarios you may encounter in life, then begin to identify who will help you navigate those situations, what resources they would need to assist you, where those resources will come from, and when specific steps should be implemented.

There are two main categories of questions that must be considered in order to determine which estate planning options make sense for you.

General questions regarding death

You must determine who the most appropriate people are in your life to take responsibility for your assets and health care, planning in the event that you are unable to do so, and how well prepared they are to do those jobs. Therefore, start your self-assessment by asking:

1. Who is best suited to step in and administer your estate should something happen to you (i.e., at incapacity or death)? Create a family tree and see if there is someone on it who has the skills needed to make decisions about your assets and medical affairs—including the requisite amount of time, experience, and knowledge. If you're like many Americans with aging parents, you may have had to assume some of these responsibilities yourself at some point. If so, think about the challenges you faced with them—what worked well, and where you struggled.

Consider a candidate's location, too. He or she should be close enough to you geographically to administer your estate without incurring undue hardship due to travel, if possible.

If you are unable to identify someone to handle these responsibilities, entities such as independent trust companies and licensed fiduciaries may be good alternatives. These options will be explored later in this chapter.

2. If the above mentioned person (or trustee) is unable to serve, who would be your second choice to administer your estate? Many people don't identify a backup person to help them if needed. But what if your first choice got a job transfer, for example, and was not easily available? Do you have any other family or friends in the area you trust enough to manage your finances and your health care on your behalf? If so, consider the age and health of that person. Giving authority to someone who is the same age as you (or older) could backfire if that person becomes incapacitated or dies before you do.

3. Why are the above mentioned people (or trustee) a good choice to administer your estate? List the reasons why you have selected the person. What qualities and skills do you feel they possess that make them ideal candidates? Writing these statements down on paper will help to clarify your thinking and provide a "gut check" that you are not overlooking a better option.

4. Do the above mentioned people have immediate access to cash to handle expenses associated with your incapacity or death? This is often overlooked. The person you choose to oversee your affairs will likely need to have access to some of your assets to pay costs associated with incapacitation (assisted living, home health care aid, groceries, bills, and so on) or death (funeral-related costs).

There are a few ways to provide for access to cash, such as setting up a payable on death (POD) designation on one of your bank accounts. POD accounts are created by filling out the proper forms at your bank or credit union. They allow for the transfer of a checking or savings account, security deposit, savings bond, or other deposit certificate. It therefore offers a quick way to disperse assets to your chosen trustee. You might also set up a joint bank account with the person you choose and fund it with just enough to cover the estimated immediate health care and funeral costs that you think would be incurred. Keep in mind, however, that all account holders in a joint account have full access to the money at any time. If you choose this option, make sure that you trust the other account holder(s) to be responsible with the money, and do not overfund the account. That way, you minimize the risk of their withdrawing money for non-estate-planning purposes. (Bonus: By holding only what you need in the account, you'll also reduce the joint account holder's potential income tax exposure.)

5. What concerns, if any, do you have about passing assets to heirs? Some families have members who are not equipped to handle an inheritance well. Others worry about the impact that a sudden influx of money could have on the motivation of younger family members to succeed and engage in hard work. It's smart to consider your likely heirs and what would happen if your assets went to them after you are gone. If you have concerns and are setting up trusts or guardianship arrangements, you might want to limit the ability of certain heirs to access assets based on requirements for how they spend the money.

6. Do you have assets or things you would like to leave to specific people? Family fights over items of great monetary or sentimental value are commonplace when the family patriarch or matriarch becomes incapacitated or dies. Designating clearly who gets what and the reasons behind your choices—through a will or other document—helps to circumvent such family squabbles.

7. Should any of your beneficiaries predecease you, do you want their allocated assets to remain with that family (for example, pass to their children)? Think about where you want assets to go if, for example, your son and daughter-in-law die before you do. Would you want these assets that were earmarked for them to transfer to their children? Or to their surviving siblings?

8. Do you foresee any of your choices creating conflicts or strains within your family? Spotting potential conflicts among family members reacting to your wishes can help you decide whether you want to head off such problems—and, if so, how to create a plan that promotes as much family harmony as possible.

9. Do you have any philanthropic goals? If so, are there charitable organizations you would like to support?

10. If you are part of a family business, do you have a succession plan in place? Family-run businesses need to identify successors to help ensure business continuity. A good succession plan also makes sure that any family members who do not want to be actively involved in the business don't get saddled with managerial or operational responsibilities.

The simple act of asking yourself these questions can clarify where you want your assets to go, who should be involved in making those decisions, and how and when to transfer assets.

Questions regarding incompetency

Many people don't realize that they are much more likely to become disabled and incompetent as the result of a trauma or accident than they are to die from it. For that matter, simply getting older can cause a reduction in mental and physical competence. It's imperative to deal with these realities in your estate planning.

In this area, it helps to ask "who, what, when, and how." For example, if you become incapacitated (short or long term), you would need to answer the following questions:

1. Who do you want legally empowered to handle your financial affairs?
2. Who do you want legally authorized to make decisions regarding your health care and end-of-life questions?
3. Who is best suited to help you with daily activities while you recover (such as eating, bathing, dressing, toileting, and taking you to medical appointments and the grocery store)?
4. Who is best suited to be a guardian—someone to help you provide day-to-day care for any dependents, such as children or parents?
5. Will any dependents or beneficiaries have special needs?
6. Who is best suited to help you maintain your household—including taking care of your pets and paying your bills?
7. If the above mentioned people are unable to serve in that capacity, who would be your second choice?

Decisions you will make when you fill out and sign advanced medical directives help guide your physicians and others about life-sustaining treatment you do (or don't) want if you are unable to communicate those wishes on your own. For example:

1. Do you wish to receive feeding tubes and water if you are terminally ill (and, if so, for what length of time)?

2. Do you want heroic measures, such as the use of artificial breathing machines, to be taken to keep you alive if it has been determined that there is no brain function occurring?

3. If you are terminal, do you want "comfort care" only—treatment meant to enhance your quality of life without artificially prolonging it?

4. Do you want to donate your organs for transplants or medical research?

CHOOSING A TRUSTEE

Many estate plans include some assets that are held in a trust or will be placed in trust after death. You may have already established one.

A trust is, at its core, a legal document or contract between the trustmaker (the person who establishes the trust—such as you and your spouse) and a trustee (the person or licensed company the trustmaker appoints to oversee the trust assets and follow the provisions listed in the trust document). In the document, the trustmaker gives the trustee written instructions about holding and administering trust assets for the benefit of the trust's beneficiaries. Think of a trust as a rulebook, and the trustee as the manager required to follow those rules. It's important to note that the trustmaker and trustee can be the same person. For example, you may serve as the trustee while you are alive. A successor trustee will then inherit your responsibilities and carry out the trust provisions after your death.

One of the most important considerations when working with trusts is to select a trustee with the appropriate experience and qualifications to handle both the administration and management of your estate.

There are three choices, each with advantages and disadvantages:

1. A family member. The advantage here is familiarity. No one knows your values and beliefs better than a member of your family, which generally fits such a person well for managing your trust estate. They have a vested interest in seeing your needs and wishes addressed in a caring and loving manner. Even though family members are permitted to charge a trustee fee, they typically do not do so or are reimbursed only for expenses. In that case, fees are lower than with other trustee arrangements.

That said, family members may be inexperienced and unfamiliar with complex financial management issues. If the trustee makes mistakes, he or she may not have the financial resources to cover the losses they cause and may imperil their own finances as a result. What's more, family relationships can be tested and may become strained or even ruined if the trustee's decisions do not sit well with his or her siblings or other relatives. Your original wishes might not be honored, or a power struggle could ensue.

2. A corporate trustee. Corporate trustees offer an objective, unemotional perspective. Managing trusts is their business, and you can expect professionalism as well as investment, tax, and estate administration expertise. They are heavily regulated by government agencies and have the financial resources to cover any mistakes they make. They also offer the benefits of continuity and stability. For example, there are no turnover issues (institutions don't die or become incapacitated, as can occur with family members serving as trustees). If they go out of business, another firm assumes their obligations.

However, corporate trustees come with complex and costly fee structures. They also may be obligated to use their internal investment departments, regardless of performance. Having a corporate fiduciary act as both trustee and investment manager could create a conflict of interest. Also, because assets may be transferred into newly created accounts when you become incapacitated or die, your family can suffer needless disruption at an emotional and difficult time. In addition, depending on the trust company selected, your other trusted professional advisors may not be able to retain their established roles in the process. That said, some corporate trustees have business structures that would allow your advisors to be retained. Your wealth manager should be well-versed in these options and should guide you through the advantages and disadvantages of working with corporate trustees.

3. Professional licensed fiduciary. This type of trustee offers numerous benefits, from typical trustee services to medical care management, moving and bill paying arrangements, and relocation assistance. Most are willing to work with real estate or alternative assets. They are usually local and available to meet personally with clients and beneficiaries, developing a relationship before their services are needed. Licensed fiduciaries can work with the client's existing advisors, preserving an established team approach to estate management.

Cost is a potential obstacle, although generally lower than bank or trust company fees. While the fiduciary business entity exists in perpetuity, the firm's personnel may turn over, and just as with corporate trustees, if a fiduciary business closes, its accounts would be transferred to another licensed and qualified fiduciary. If you explore this option, be sure you are working with an established professional fiduciary that is licensed. In Arizona, for example, fiduciaries are licensed through the Arizona Supreme Court.

THE FOUNDATION FOR SUCCESS

These questions and issues are the same ones that I discuss with clients as we work together and with other professionals to create estate plans. I encourage you to reflect on them.

CHAPTER 11

Advanced Planning Strategy
#3: Insurance Planning

By this stage of your life, you understand the importance of insurance. The ability to protect yourself and those you care about is vital to your financial well-being and your peace of mind.

That said, families often are overwhelmed by the topic of insurance—and they overlook types of insurance that may be beneficial to them. Everyone knows they need auto, homeowners, and health insurance. But what about policies to cover disabilities, long-term care needs, and death of a primary wage earner? What about insurance aimed at protecting valuable possessions, such as art? In chapter 12, we will cover umbrella insurance policies designed to protect people against lawsuits from accidents and negligence from family members.

This chapter gives you a framework for assessing risks you face and formulating responses to them. As with previous chapters, this isn't a deep analysis of specific insurance vehicles. The goal here is to help you think about risk-related issues that should inform your insurance decisions. Your advisors can discuss the answers to these questions and then implement strategies that are informed by your foundational work.

ASSESSING AND RESPONDING TO RISK

Like virtually everything else in wealth management, insurance decisions should be guided by a systematic process. In this case, that involves following five steps:

Step 1: Think about your objectives.

As was done in the discovery meeting for investments, your insurance assessment should begin by clarifying your objectives. Each person's situation is unique, but chances are your risk-related goals include some variation of the following:

- To protect yourself and/or your family from catastrophic financial loss due to short- or long-term disability, disease, or the aging process, or premature death.
- To preserve the existing roles that you and your family members now hold, so that those roles are not disrupted by a catastrophic event. For example, a stay-at-home mother can continue to be a stay-at-home mother, and any minor children can continue with their schools, interests, and aspirations.
- To protect your financial independence and ensure that you not become a burden to your family due to health concerns or cognitive issues as you age.
- To identify tools to mitigate these risks, at costs that are reasonable and within your budget.

Step 2: Identify the specific risks you and your family face.

Once you understand your broad-based objectives, consider the hazards you face or are likely to face down the road. For example:

- Actuarially speaking, you are about three and a half times more likely to be injured and need disability coverage than you are to die and need life insurance.[5]
- For men reaching the age of sixty-five in 2005, 17 percent will need some level of long-term care for two to five years. And another 11 percent will have a need that is more than five years.[6]
- For women reaching the age of sixty-five in 2005, 22 percent will need some level of long-term care for two to five years. And a further 28 percent will have a need that is more than five years.[7]

Start by re-examining the budget you developed (see chapter 7) and estimating how it might be affected if you encounter various health-related risks. If you suffer a long-term disability that leaves you incapacitated, for example, you might find that some of your costs decline or are eliminated (such as the need for a second automobile). Other costs may increase (such as modifications made to your home).

To assist you in this task, the budget worksheet from chapter 7 is included here again.

BUDGETING WORKSHEET

Expense Description	Monthly Expense	Yearly Expense
Primary Residence:		
Mortgage Payment (Principal and Interest Only)		
Property Taxes		
Home Insurance		
Average Electric		
Average Water/Sewer		
Average Phone		
Average Fuel or Gas		
Trash Removal		
Cable, Internet, TV		
Homeowners Assoc. Dues		
Misc. Maintenance		
Other		
Other		
Second Residence:		
Mortgage Payment (Principal and Interest Only)		
Property Taxes		
Home Insurance		
Average Electric		
Average Water/Sewer		
Average Phone		
Average Fuel or Gas		
Trash Removal		
Cable, Internet, TV		
Homeowners Assoc. Dues		
Misc. Maintenance		
Other		
Other		
Investment Property:		
Mortgage Payment (Principal and Interest Only)		
Property Taxes		
Property Insurance		
Maintenance Expense		
Property Management Fee		
Homeowners Assoc. Dues		
Other		

Expense Description	Monthly Expense	Yearly Expense
Insurance:		
Health Insurance		
Dental Insurance		
Life Insurance		
Long Term Care Insurance		
Disability Insurance		
Umbrella Insurance		
Auto Insurance		
Auto Insurance		
Auto Insurance		
Other Insurance		
Other Insurance		
Automobiles:		
Payment 1		
Payment 2		
Payment 3		
Gas/Oil		
Maintenance/Repairs		
Annual Licensing		
Car Wash		
Other		
Other		
Groceries, Food, Leisure:		
Groceries		
Meals Outside Home		
Other Misc Food Expenses		
Travel/Vacation		
Entertainment		
Other Credit Card		
Clothing:		
Purchase		
Cleaning/Repair		
Other		
Gifts/Charity:		
Holiday Gifts		
Birthday Gifts		
Church		
Charity		
Other		
Other		

Expense Description	Monthly Expense	Yearly Expense
Professional Fees:		
Physician		
Dental		
Eye Care		
Hair Stylist		
Accountant		
Attorney		
Veterinarian		
Other		
Miscellaneous:		
Health Club		
House Cleaning		
School/College		
Child Care		
Wedding		
Funeral Expenses		
Other		
Other		
Loans/Debt Payments:		
Credit Card		
Recreational Vehicle		
Home Equity Line of Credit		
Educational Loans		
Other		
Extraordinary: Auto Replacement		
Total Estimated Tax (Rate Assumption 20%)		
Gross Annual Income Need in Retirement (GAINR)		

* Figure rounded.

If you form a relatively clear picture of the financial impact that these and other risks could have on your budget, you can begin to answer the important questions. Here are some.

Questions about disability:

1. If you or a family member incurred a short-term disability (defined as ninety days or less), would your financial resources be sufficient to support your predisability lifestyle?

2. If you or a family member incurred a long-term disability (defined as three to twenty-four months), would your financial resources be sufficient to support your predisability lifestyle?

3. If you or a family member suffered a permanent disability (defined as greater than two years), how long would financial resources last before affecting your predisability lifestyle?

4. If you or any family member is a business owner and were to be disabled for any amount of time, are adequate succession plans in place, or would the company's future be in jeopardy? Would that affect your personal finances?

5. If you or a family member incurred a disability, would you or they qualify for benefits from

- employer-paid disability insurance?
- Social Security disability benefits?
- individual disability income insurance policies?
- Workers Compensation or another form of insurance policy?

6. If you have a disability insurance policy, what are the details? In the accompanying table, you will find a hypothetical example of a typical disability policy. The information in the table will help you see the details you will want to gather to help you understand the coverage you may have.

DISABILITY INSURANCE PLANNING

Disability Insurance Policy Information	Details
Insurance Company Name:	Acme Insurance Co.
Policy Number:	ABC1234
Policy Owner(s):	Bob Smith
Insured's Name:	Bob Smith
Beneficiary:	Bob Smith
Policy Inception Date:	January 1, 2014
Insured's Age at Policy Inception Date:	50
Annual Premium Payment:	$1,600
Elimination Period:	90 days
Maximum Monthly Benefit:	$4,000
Maximum Benefit Period:	5 Years up to age 65
Policy includes Annual Inflation Adjustment:	Yes
Definition of Disability:	Perform own occupation
Does policy include Death Benefit:	Yes, $12,000
Employer-Paid, or Individually Paid Policy?	Individual
If benefits are paid, are they subject to tax?	No
Other Policy Information:	

Questions about death:

1. If you or a family member died, could you or your surviving family members maintain their lifestyle and see to future financial needs, or would this be a financial catastrophe? (For example, would your house have to be sold?)

2. If you or a family member died, would the estate be subject to federal and state death taxes? If so, are financial resources available to pay the tax liability?

3. If you or any family member is a business owner and were to die, are adequate succession plans in place—or would the company's future be in jeopardy? How would a succession crisis affect your personal finances?

4. If you have one or more life insurance policies, what are their details? In the accompanying table, Life Insurance Planning, you will find a hypothetical example to prompt you for the type of information to gather to help you understand the coverage you may have.

LIFE INSURANCE PLANNING

Life Insurance Policy Information	Details
Insurance Company Name:	Acme Insurance Co.
Policy Number:	DEF5678
Policy Owner(s):	Bob Smith
Insured's Name:	Bob Smith
Beneficiary:	Mary Smith
Policy Inception Date:	January 1, 2014
Death Benefit:	$2,000,000
Insured's Age at Policy Inception Date:	50
Annual Premium Payment:	$10,000
Type of Policy: Term or Permanent:	Permanent (Whole Life)
If Permanent Policy, Total Cash Value:	$100,000
If Permanent Policy, Total Investment Gain in Policy:	$30,000
Other Policy Information:	

Questions about long-term care needs:

Long-term health care has become a serious concern for millions of Americans—in particular the baby boomer generation, which has been entering (or soon will enter) retirement. Consider these statistics from Genworth Financial about the projected costs of long-term health care in the Phoenix area:

Monthly cost of a home health aide
In 2014: $3,861
By 2044: $9,372

Monthly cost of an assisted living facility (private, one bedroom)
   In 2014: $3,000
   By 2044: $7,282

Monthly cost of nursing home care (private room)
   In 2014: $7,239
   By 2044: $17,571

(Note: The 2044 estimates assume annualized rate of increase of 3 percent.)

You can use this type of cost information to answer the following questions and make informed decisions about whether it makes sense to take out a long-term care policy and, if so, how large a policy you need.

1. If you or a family member needed long-term care (defined by an inability to perform two or more activities of daily living—bathing or showering, dressing, eating, mobility, continence, and dressing—for longer than ninety days), are sufficient resources available for home care, assisted living, or nursing home care? Would the money last longer than five years?

2. If you or a family member suffered a deterioration of mental capacity (defined as a person's inability to make their own choices and function cognitively), are sufficient financial resources available to provide and care for this person? Would those resources last longer than five years?

3. If you have a long-term care policy, what are its details? In the accompanying table, Long-Term Care Planning, you will find a

hypothetical example that will help you see the type of information you will want to gather to help you understand any coverage you may have.

LONG-TERM CARE PLANNING

Long-Term Care Insurance Policy Information	Details
Insurance Company Name:	Acme Insurance Co.
Policy Number:	GHI9999
Policy Owner(s):	Bob Smith
Insured's Name:	Bob Smith
Beneficiary:	Bob Smith
Policy Inception Date:	January 1, 2014
Daily Benefit:	$150.00
Insured's Age:	50
Annual Premium Payment:	$2,400
Elimination Period:	20 Days
Total Benefit Period:	5 Years
Policy Includes Annual Inflation Adjustment?	Yes
Additional Riders:	

Questions about specialized risks you may face:

1. Do you own valuable artwork, classic cars, antiques, or other high-value collectibles?

2. Do you live in a flood plain, and does your homeowners insurance cover damage from floods and flood-related events? (Many policies do not.)

3. Do you live in an area where earthquakes are common events? If so, do you have insurance to cover quake damage?

4. Do you travel extensively? Does that include overseas locations? In particular, do you travel to any global hot spots that present above-average risks?

5. Are you an active member of any boards of directors or corporate, community, or neighborhood association? If so, does the organization carry director and officer insurance, and does it cover you?

6. Do you have any policies in force that cover the specialized risks? If so, what are the details? (In chapter 12, Asset Protection, we review umbrella liability insurance coverage.)

To help you answer these questions, see the Risk Matrix below, following Step 5. You also may wish to review the foregoing questions with financial professionals you work with.

Step 3: Consider methods of addressing the risks.

In general, there are three main strategies for coping with financial risk:

- **Retain the risk.** You may be equipped to manage certain risks out of your existing financial resources and therefore not need insurance for those risks. An example would be if you have real estate holdings that you could (and would be willing to) sell in order to pay for disability or long-term care needs.
- **Transfer the risk.** This, of course, is the whole point of having insurance policies—to transfer risk from yourself to the insurance company.
- **Share the risk.** This approach takes a middle ground between the previous two options, transferring some risk to the insurance company while you retain some yourself, counting

on your own financial resources. This approach can be a good option when the cost of fully insuring against a risk is prohibitively high. It also can make sense if you have sources of income that can help cover certain costs. For example, you may decide that some pension and Social Security income could be used to pay for a portion of long-term care expenses, if necessary, and make up any gap using a relatively small insurance policy.

Step 4: Implement the strategy

After coordination with your financial professionals, you implement your strategy. This involves purchasing the appropriate insurance policy if you decide to transfer or share a risk.

Working with a professional wealth manager and insurance advisor to select the best insurance policy is the most appropriate step to take when you choose to transfer risk. If you choose to retain a risk and not use insurance, you'll be guided to identify the assets that will be used to cover it.

Step 5: Evaluate and review regularly.

New risks may arise in your life as your situation changes, while old risks may decline or disappear. For example, in 2001 (and made permanent in 2003), Congress significantly increased the federal estate tax exemption. The need for life insurance policies to cover estate tax liabilities was reduced or eliminated for many investors. Conversely, as you become older, the need for long-term care insurance may rise if you encounter new health problems.

The changeability of health care laws and policies is one of the biggest reasons to conduct regular reviews. As conditions change, and as your own health situation changes, you may find that a high-premium/low-out-of-pocket policy makes more sense than a policy with an extremely low monthly premium that essentially requires you to pay for most services from your wallet. These complexities are becoming an increasingly important part of discussions about retirement planning and budgeting.

What's more, new types of insurance offerings are being created on a fairly regular basis—especially as the huge wave of baby boomers continue to enter their traditional retirement years. New products could provide you with better coverage or lower costs.

One of the most important things you should review is your beneficiary designations. As discussed in chapter 3, beneficiary designations help ensure that your assets—including insurance policy benefits—go the people, charities, or trusts of your choosing when the time comes. If your situation changes—divorce, remarriage, new circumstances of your heirs, and so on—your insurance policies must be updated to reflect any new wishes you have regarding the distribution of your assets.

And here's something to keep in mind: An insurance review can identify mistakes that have been made with existing policies, so that corrective actions can be taken. Often when clients first meet with our firm, we discover that they have insurance policies for which they are paying too much or that they simply no longer need.

THE RISK MATRIX

As you ask yourself all these questions, write your answers in the following risk matrix. This framework will help you see the risks you do and don't face, and their potential impact to your financial and emotional well-being. With this information in hand, you'll get more out of your work with your insurance professional and wealth manager as they help you formulate the right plan.

Here's an example to get you started.

- Say you incurred a short-term disability that put you out of work for ninety days. How much money do you estimate you would need to get through that period of time?
- Let's assume the answer is $40,000 in lost income and additional expenses. This is the potential size of the loss if the risk occurred.
- Next, examine the amount of money you have on hand to cover this expense. Based on that, how would you assess the level of risk that such a disability would present?
- For example, if you have nowhere near $40,000 in cash or marketable holdings, you might determine this to be a high-risk event that could cause a financial catastrophe. In that case, disability insurance is likely to be a necessary purchase. That said, if you have well over $40,000 in liquid assets in an emergency fund, a short-term disability might be a low-risk event that would not require you to insure yourself against it.
- Finally, as you shop around for a policy, you would want to decide if the cost of the policy is within your budget.

RISK MATRIX

RISK	What is the potential size of the loss if the risk event occurred?	This is high risk resulting in financial catastrophe. (Transfer risk to insurance company)	This is a moderate risk resulting in financial hardship. (Consider sharing risk with insurance company)	This is a low risk resulting in no financial hardship or catastrophe. (Retain risk, no insurance needed.)	Is the cost of insurance solution reasonable and within my budget?
Short Term Disability (90 days or less)					
Long Term Disability (lasting 3 months to 2 years)					
Permanent Disability (2 years or more)					
Death of Family Member					
Death of Family Member who is business owner and Impact on company/family					
Individual or family member experiences long-term care event					
Individual or family member begins to have mental deterioration or cognitive issues requiring care					
I or a family member who is business owner experiences long-term care event or mental deterioration or cognitive issue					
If I or various family members died, would the estate incur federal and state death taxes?					
Do I have specialized risks due to owning expensive artwork, living in a flood plain, traveling frequently to volatile parts of the world, etc.?					

The insurance review process in this chapter is designed to help you anticipate many risks you may face in life. Addressing potential losses before they occur will ensure your wealth management goals remain in place.

CHAPTER 12

Advanced Planning Strategy #4: Asset Protection

Take a minute to consider the wealth you have worked diligently to build and maintain over your lifetime. If you have inherited money, think about the efforts that your family undertook to grow those assets and ensure that they would be there for you.

Now ask yourself, "What would happen if someone tried to take that wealth from my family and me?"

Asset protection aims to ward off threats and scenarios that could cause you to lose much or all of what you have. Such threats include divorce, actions taken by creditors, lawsuits from individuals or business partners, serious accidents that you or family members have (or cause), and identity theft.

Protecting wealth is a growing concern among many investors and their families, especially those with significant wealth. And no wonder: The number of lawsuits against business owners—including wage disputes and labor-related lawsuits—has risen sharply in recent years.

That means it's time to think about safeguarding your wealth from those who could take it. This chapter will spell out the need for asset protection, help you determine your level of exposure, and describe some strategies for protecting wealth. That said, a detailed analysis of specific types of asset protection vehicles is beyond the scope of a single chapter in this or any book. Your advisors should consult with you to help answer the questions that appear below and to begin formulating appropriate responses.

THE NEED FOR ASSET PROTECTION

Asset protection planning often involves taking steps to minimize— or even eliminate—the risk that creditors and other claimants could reach your assets. There's no question that the risk can be enormous. Consider these eye-opening facts:

- Each year, more than 15 million civil lawsuits are filed in the United States.[8]
- The annual cost to the US economy for civil lawsuits exceeds $230 billion.[9]
- Of the tort trials in the United States, plaintiffs win more than 50 percent.[10]
- Nearly one out of six jury awards is for more than $1 million.[11]

The threat of lawsuits is a surprisingly broad. They can take many forms. For example:

1. Professional liability. Professionals such as doctors, accountants, and Realtors face professional liability risks. A physician, for example, might be sued by a patient due to the outcome of a particular procedure. It's estimated that over $3 billion is spent in medical malpractice payouts a year.[12]

2. Business owner/executive risk. Business owners without the proper planning in place can be financially wiped out if they are successfully sued for negligence. You as the owner could be sued if your executives or employees make bad business decisions or take illegal actions. Consider the firm with an employee who stole customers' credit card information. The owners had to pay for ID theft protection services for their entire client base—at a cost of $800,000.

3. Business litigation. Lawsuits may occur among partners within a business or as a result of failed business or real estate deals.

4. Family liability. Car accidents, injuries incurred on property you own (homes, cabins, swimming pools), and divorce all can lead to situations where assets are put in jeopardy.

5. Creditors. If you don't pay your bills or if you declare bankruptcy, creditors may take actions to get the money they are owed. Creditors with secured claims—such as mortgages and car loans—can foreclose on your property. Creditors with unsecured claims—credit card debt, medical bills, and so on—may sue you and try to enforce a judgment against you by taking whatever assets they can get.

In addition to lawsuits, identity theft is becoming a threat to asset protection that must be taken seriously. According to the Federal Trade Commission, the personal information of roughly 9 million Americans is stolen annually.

The goal of an ID thief is to use your information to commit fraud and steal assets. Their methods range from traditional theft to technology-enabled strategies. For example:

1. Stealing. The most basic way that thieves access sensitive personal and financial information is to steal wallets, purses, and mail.

2. Trash/dumpster-diving. ID thieves go through people's garbage, looking for bills and other documents with sensitive personal and financial information.

3. Phishing. Online data thieves send emails purporting to come from banks and other financial institutions. These emails request that recipients send their personal information or that they log in to a bogus lookalike website using a hyperlink embedded in the email. Some of these emails are artful counterfeits of alerts and notices you're used to seeing from accounts you manage online, and they are easy to mistake for authentic messages.

4. Hacking and other breaches. If a company's website is compromised or other technology systems are hacked, data thieves may be able to gain access to personal information or financial accounts.

ASSESSING YOUR RISK EXPOSURE

Just as with your estate planning efforts, your first step with asset protection is to conduct a self-assessment so you understand your exposure. Consider the following questions:

- Do you own or are you a partner in a business? How is the business titled?
- Are you in a profession that is high-risk for lawsuits (examples include physicians, attorneys, and architects)?
- Do you own car, boat, plane, or other leisure-time assets in your own name?
- Do you own a brokerage account in your own name or the name of your spouse?

- Do you have equity of more than $150,000 in your primary residence?
- Do you own real estate other than your home (such as rental property or commercial property), in your own name or your spouse's name? How is it titled?
- Do you own any other assets of high value owned in your or your spouse's personal name (antiques, collectibles, art work, jewelry)?
- Do you have dependent children living at home? Do they have a license to drive a car? (Parents can be100 percent liable for their dependent children's actions.)
- Do you have concerns about the health of the relationships that any of your children are in? Do you worry about the possibility of divorce?
- Do you keep sensitive information such as your Social Security card in your wallet or purse?
- Do you shop or conduct banking online or use your computer to check financial statements?
- Are your passwords to websites written down on paper and located in an obvious or easy-to-find location?

EXPLORING ASSET PROTECTION STRATEGIES

The most important step is to start early. There is very little you can do to safeguard your wealth once a claim is filed or liability occurs.

1. Take advantage of natural asset protection. Some of your assets can be held (and likely already are being held) in vehicles that can't be touched by creditors. Some examples:

- Homestead property. In Arizona, for example, up to $150,000 in a home's equity is protected from creditor claims and lawsuits.
- IRAs (other than inherited IRAs), pension plans, and 401(k) accounts. These types of retirement accounts are 100 percent protected from creditors (though they may not be exempted from some divorce settlement actions), except for contributions made during the previous 120 days (specific to State of Arizona law. Consult legal advisor for your specific state's statute). Therefore, it may make sense to maximize contributions to these types of plans.
- Annuities. These accounts are 100 percent protected as long as they have been in place for at least two years and the beneficiaries are blood relatives.
- Life insurance policies. These policies are 100 percent protected as long as the policy has been in place for at least two years.

2. Take out the right liability insurance. Liability insurance, including home and auto insurance, as well as personal umbrella policies, pay costs above and beyond those covered by the more common types of liability insurance. For example, umbrella policies might cover bodily injuries suffered by someone visiting your home or damage to property. Read your policies and know what the limits are, what is covered—and what is not covered .A thorough review of your insurance coverage will tell you where there may be risky gaps. Conversely, you might find that some existing policies provide excessive coverage or are entirely unnecessary due to changes in your lifestyle.

3. Title any business entities properly. Businesses should be operated through their own separate entities—such as a corporation, limited partnership, or limited liability company—so that your personal assets are not exposed in the event your business gets sued. In a limited partnership, for example, a creditor may not be able to access the partnership's underlying assets and can get paid only if the partnership makes distributions. Each type of entity has advantages and disadvantages that go beyond asset protection concerns to involve tax-related issues and other factors. Your accountant and attorney can review your situation to determine the best option for your business.

4. Set up one or more trusts designed to protect assets. By transferring ownership of an asset to an *irrevocable trust*—that is, one in which your gift to the trust can't be taken back—you make it more difficult for creditors to claim the assets. The reason is that the irrevocable trust technically owns the asset, not you. Parents who plan to leave an inheritance to their children also can set up trusts to stop children's spouses from getting at that money in the event of a divorce. There are numerous types of irrevocable trusts to consider when planning specific strategies with a CPA or estate planning attorney. In addition, asset protection trusts can be set up in jurisdictions where laws are more favorable to investors and business owners than to creditors. These include both domestic jurisdictions (such as South Dakota) and foreign jurisdictions (including Bermuda and the Cayman Islands).

5. Take steps to protect your identify. Simple steps can shut down some of the biggest threats here. Don't carry sensitive personal information such as your Social Security number or passport with you. Don't give out your Social Security number unless absolutely necessary—and never in response to an unsolicited phone call or email. Even if you call a merchant or service provider yourself, use your account number or other information as a way to verify your identity, instead of your Social Security number. In addition, buy a paper shredder and put account statements and other financial documents through it before throwing them away.

Don't send your financial information using email. Instead, only send it over a secure Internet connection (such as a website that begins with the letters "https"). And install and regularly update protective software such as antivirus, antispam, and antimalware software. Don't use obvious passwords (such as abc123 or your name) for your online accounts, and keep any written lists of your passwords stored securely.

If you know—or even suspect—that your identity has been stolen, call the three credit reporting agencies and tell them to place a fraud alert on your credit reports. That tells credit card companies to follow certain procedures before opening new cards in your name or making changes to your existing cards. Here ae phone numbers for the three agencies:

- **Equifax**: (800) 685-1111 (general) or (800) 525-6285 (fraud)
- **Experian**: (888) 397-3742 (general and fraud)
- **TransUnion**: (800) 888-4213 (general) or (800) 680-7289 (fraud)

If any accounts have been compromised or established without your consent, close them immediately by calling each company's fraud department. Then file a police report so you can show creditors proof of the theft.

ASSET PROTECTION IN ACTION

To see how asset protection strategies can work, consider the following hypothetical example of a couple with a net worth of $7 million. Their assets are divided among the following categories:

Annuities: $1,000,000
IRAs: $3,000,000
Revocable trusts: $1,000,000
Real estate equity: $1,000,000
Life insurance cash value: $750,000
Gold coins: $200,000
Bank accounts: $50,000

As seen in the accompanying table, Asset Protection in Action, much of that $7 million is sheltered from creditors and lawsuits, including the annuities, the IRAs, the life insurance cash value, and up to $150,000 of real estate equity. The result: Only approximately $2.1 million of their $7 million in total assets is exposed to creditors.

The couple has a $2 million umbrella insurance policy and a $500,000 automobile liability policy. These would help cover a judgment against the couple's remaining exposure, assuming the incident is covered. The couple's next step would be to consider risks not covered by the umbrella policy and identify which, if any, asset protection strategies are necessary to defend against them.

ASSET PROTECTION IN ACTION

Account	Total Account Balance or Asset Value	Creditor Protected	Non-Creditor Protected
Individual Retirement Accounts (IRA)	$3,000,000	$3,000,000	$0
Annuities	$1,000,000	$1,000,000	$0
Revocable Family Trust Account	$1,000,000	$0	$1,000,000
Real Estate Equity in Primary Residence	$1,000,000	$150,000	$850,000
Life Insurance Cash Value	$750,000	$750,000	$0
Gold Coins	$200,000	$0	$200,000
Bank Accounts	$50,000	$0	$50,000
Total	$7,000,000	$4,900,000	$2,100,000

WORK TOGETHER TO MAKE INTELLIGENT DECISIONS

Clearly, asset protection is a big topic that can involve things as basic as using a paper shredder and as complex as creating trusts in non-US jurisdictions. What's more, rules involving asset protection strategies often vary from state to state. To ensure you make intelligent decisions that are relevant to your situation, you will want to work with a team of advisors that includes a financial advisor, an attorney, a tax advisor, and an insurance specialist. There are many areas of your financial life that you can take full control of, but asset protection demands the coordinated effort of a team of experts who can guide you and ensure that your assets remain exactly where you want them.

CHAPTER 13

Advanced Planning Strategy #4: Charitable Giving

Philanthropy is an issue of growing importance for investors at all levels of wealth. In the United States, total giving to charitable organizations amounts to more than $300 billion annually. Most of that money—around 70 percent—comes from individuals such as yourself.[13] From religious organizations and educational institutions to human services groups and arts and environmental causes, investors seek to use their wealth in ways large and small to impact the world positively.

On the surface, engaging in philanthropy seems simple: Choose a cause, find a charity, and send money. However, effective charitable giving requires great thought and care. When you consider that approximately 1.4 million nonprofit organizations operate in the United States alone,[14] it's easy to see that giving *intelligently* is a challenge if you are charitably inclined.

As the purpose of this book is to help you make more informed decisions about your wealth, this chapter will set forth some issues you should consider when formulating a charitable plan. You will want to consult with any trusted advisors you work with (financial, tax, attorney) to determine together the approaches best suited to you.

A PROCESS FOR PHILANTHROPIC SUCCESS

You can use the following seven-step process to guide your philanthropic decisions:

Step 1: Define your broad mission.

Start by taking a high-level view of giving. Think broadly about what you might want some of your wealth to accomplish. Review the values that you identified during your discovery meeting (see chapter 1). This is an opportunity to crystallize your thinking about what matters to you and what you want your money to support.

As an exercise to gain clarity, write down your answers to the following five questions:

1. What are your passions?
2. What inspires you?
3. What good would you like to achieve?
4. Are you religious, and do you want your faith to be reflected in your philanthropic goals?
5. How important is family involvement in your philanthropy?

Some answers to these questions might come quickly. Others might require a little rumination. If you have been personally affected by a disease, for example—say a family member had cancer—you may decide that the good you want to achieve is helping to cure cancer or develop better cancer treatments. Or you might have a passion for learning and want to see disadvantaged children have greater access to books and other educational resources.

You might consider using your philanthropic efforts to instill values like caring and empathy in your children or grandchildren, and teach them lessons about financial choices and decision-making as well. Children who take part in family philanthropy can see how wealth is a tool not just for acquiring things and having fun but also for giving back to the community and making a positive difference in people's lives. They also can see how fortunate they are by engaging with those in need.

Step 2: Hone in on your mission.

There are numerous, diverse types of charitable entities that you can give to in order to achieve your broad philanthropic mission. Go deeper in this area by reflecting on these questions:

1. What entities would you like to support? Options include

- direct service to individuals,
- scholarships (specific or general grants),
- universities or other educational institutions,
- community services (food banks, health care initiatives),
- medical facilities,
- research initiatives and efforts (medical, technology, other), and
- arts organizations

2. Do you prefer to support local, regional, national, or international charitable entities? Many charities focus on effecting change on a large scale (think CARE, International Rescue Committee, or Doctors

Without Borders), while others target issues in one geographic area. For example, more than 750 community foundations exist in the United States. Each one seeks to address challenges in its local community.

3. Do you want your grant to be a large one-time gift, or multiple smaller grants made over time? Donating a significant sum all at once can create a significant impact quickly. That said, not everyone has the financial flexibility to donate large amounts in one fell swoop and may prefer to make smaller gifts on a consistent basis. Smaller gifts also enable donors to dip their toes in the water with a particular charity and see how effectively the organization uses its resources before making additional financial commitments.

4. Do you want to support entities by donating your time and expertise, or support them at a distance? Some people simply want to make financial contributions. Others wish to get involved with their chosen charity in more active ways—for example, by becoming a member of the charity's board of directors and helping to shape its mission.

5. Do you want to support a charity broadly, or fund specific initiatives within the charity? Charities often have programs that target specific issues—fighting hunger in a country or region, for example. You can ask that your gifts go to support these focused efforts, or you can donate broadly and allow the charity to use the money where they see the most need.

6. Are you looking for immediate payoffs, or do you prefer to support long-term initiatives? Some people enjoy seeing the results of their philanthropy quickly. Capital campaigns, for example, are designed to help charities raise money for projects that have specific end dates, such as the construction of a new facility or campus. Other initiatives are longer-term in nature, such as ongoing cancer research or building an endowment, and may not yield immediate results.

Step 3: Identify charities that match your mission.

As noted above, there is no shortage of charities to support. Once you define what you want your philanthropy to accomplish, you can set out to identify and evaluate specific organizations.

Start by asking friends, colleagues, and family members if they know of any charities that support your chosen cause or causes. You may know someone who is active within a charity and who can steer you in the right direction. If you work with a financial advisor or CPA, tap them for ideas and introductions to people who can help you.

Take advantage of Internet resources. There are several websites that can help you find charities that match your interests. Some of them also provide a deep level of due diligence into how each charity spends its money and other indicators that can tell you how well run the organization is. These are excellent resources for determining how effective specific charities are at realizing their missions. The fact is, some charities spend just a small percentage of the money they take in on the causes they say they support. The rest gets eaten up by high administrative and other costs.

Here are a few of the largest and most helpful sites:

- Guidestar (www.guidestar.org)
- Givewell (www.givewell.org)
- Charity Navigator (www.charitynavigator.org)

Finally, if you end up donating through a donor-advised fund (explained below under Step 5), you can ask the fund to help you locate and vet qualified charities.

Step 4: Determine your giving preferences.

Choosing the right charitable tool for your aims can be a complex process. It can be helpful to use six factors recommended by Vanguard Charitable to bring your preferences and giving goals into focus. As you consider each of their six giving preferences,[15] rank each one by importance to you—high importance, medium importance, or low importance.

1. Tax efficiency. How important is it that you receive the optimal tax deductions from your giving? Deductibility limits vary based on the asset donated, the giving option, and any personal benefit the donor derives from the gift. For example, a donation to a charitable gift annuity, which allows the donor to receive income, does not allow for as substantial a tax deduction as a direct gift. The most tax-effective assets to donate are also sometimes the most difficult—such as special assets or appreciated securities. If you're in that situation, choose a giving tool that supports liquidation of these complex assets.

2. Cost. How important is it that you keep the cost of giving as low as possible? The more money spent on fees, the less is available for charity, of course. Most giving tools charge administrative fees to cover startup, employee, and service costs. Others may charge legal or accounting expenses. Investment fees also play a crucial role in a long-term giving plan, as high expense ratios can erode returns over time and dampen your charitable impact.

3. Control or level of input. How much direct oversight and decision-making influence do you want for each area of your philanthropy—such as grant-making, investing, or administrative work? Strict legal regulations may limit your ability to exercise control with different giving tools. Some giving options permit donor input or advice without allowing the donor to exercise direct control over the assets.

4. Distribution to charity. How frequently do you wish to give? Ensure the giving tool allows you to support charitable causes in sync with your mission and, if desired, affords you the ability to give to multiple charities on a consistent basis or grant one large sum in the future.

5. Legacy giving options. Do you want your charitable giving to last beyond your own lifetime? Leaving a philanthropic legacy is a personal decision that can take various forms, from bestowing assets to others, to naming a charity as a beneficiary in a will, or continuing a family tradition of giving. Some charitable giving options—direct giving, for example—can't support specific charitable wishes and intergenerational philanthropy after a donor passes, while others can.

6. Recognition versus anonymity. Do you want your philanthropic efforts to be known and recognized? Legally, not all giving tools can be sensitive to wishes for anonymity, while some may be able to cater to specific recognition requests. For example, private foundations are required to disclose information on grants, trustees, and employees, whereas grants from an account with a donor-advised fund (see Step 5) can maintain donor confidentiality if so desired.

Step 5: Assess your charitable giving options.

There are several ways to make financial gifts to charities. In the accompanying table, Charitable Giving Options, you can see how each of these options stacks up in terms of the six key giving preferences outlined in the previous section.

CHARITABLE GIVING OPTIONS

GIVING TOOLS	Tax Efficacy*	Cost	Level of Input	Distribution to Charity	Charitable Legacy Options	Recognition versus Anonymity
Charitable Gift Annuity	Limited	Low	Minimal	Restricted	Some	Some flexibility
Charitable Remainder Trust	Limited	High	Maximum	Some restrictions	Some	Flexible
Direct Giving	Full	None	Maximum	No restrictions	None	Some flexibility
Donor-advised Fund	Full	Low	Moderate	Some restrictions	Many	Flexible
Private Foundation	Partial	High	Maximum	Some restrictions	Many	Not flexible

Source: Vanguard Charitable

Here is an overview of the various charitable giving options listed in the table.

1. Charitable gift annuity. This is a contract with a particular charity in which you make a donation and receive a limited tax deduction immediately. The charity agrees to pay you a fixed rate of return regularly over the rest of your life and then keeps the remainder of the assets after you're gone. If you donate appreciated securities such as stocks or funds directly to the charity, you won't owe capital gains tax when you make the transfer. This can be a good option if you are certain about which organization you want to support, and if you want or need a regular income stream during retirement.

2. Charitable remainder trust. You make an irrevocable gift during your lifetime to the trust and receive a limited tax deduction when you make the gift. You'll receive annual payments for your lifetime or a specific number of years. Each year, the trust is revalued, so the amount of money you receive will fluctuate. After the term ends or you pass, your chosen charity gets the remainder of the assets. As with many trusts, setup costs can be substantial.

3. Direct giving. The most obvious way to give is to make a tax-deductible gift of cash or property directly to a charity, either one time or on a recurring basis. This type of "checkbook philanthropy" gives you a high degree of control in terms of the timing and size of the gifts and your choice of charitable organization.

4. Donor-advised fund. You can set up a donor-advised fund through a mutual fund company or other provider and donate assets to it—such as cash, stocks, and mutual funds. The donation is irrevocable—meaning you can't get the asset back. However, you receive an immediate tax deduction for your gift when you make it. And you can take as much time as you want to select a specific charity that you want the money to support. In the meantime, the fund will invest that money in order to grow your pool of charitable capital and ultimately be able to grant larger sums than you might have been able to otherwise. This option comes with some cost—you will pay an annual fee for the management of the assets. Technically, you do not have control over the assets in the fund. That means you can only *recommend* which charity gets the money. (That said, a fund will almost certainly honor your recommendation, as long as it's for a charity in good standing.)

5. Private foundation. Investors with significant wealth might consider setting up their own tax-exempt nonprofit foundations to manage and implement their philanthropy. This option is the most complex—it requires annual reporting to the IRS, and the costs of starting a private foundation can exceed $10,000. This option does provide donors with the maximum level of control. It also can serve as a way to include family members in the giving process and ensure a lasting legacy.

Step 6: Consider what you want to give.

With a solid knowledge base, you can now select the best asset to give based on your evaluation above. Ask yourself how you want to fulfill your charitable mission.

Giving money or donating goods are the obvious ways to engage in philanthropy. Options include the following:

1. Cash. Cash donations are tax deductible, up to a certain percentage of your adjusted gross income.

2. Appreciated stock. As we've seen, you can donate highly appreciated shares of stock or mutual funds and take a tax deduction (again, up to certain limits). By donating stocks directly to a charity instead of selling the shares first and donating the proceeds, you will avoid paying capital gains taxes.

3. Tangible property. You can donate most types of property—including automobiles and real estate—to a charity and also receive a tax deduction.

That said, you might consider other ways to implement charitable giving:

1. Your time. Charities often need effort as much as money, and volunteering time can be a great way to support a cause that is important to you.

2. Your skills. Companies often donate their resources to charities and charitable events. For example, an advertising agency might donate a hundred hours of free ad work to promote the charity.

3. Fundraising. You might reach out to community leaders and other influential people and businesses to encourage them to give.

Depending on your level of wealth and the amount of time you have to give, a combination of these six options could strike the right balance.

Step 7: Implement and monitor.

Implementation simply means executing your plan—setting up a donor-advised fund or working with an attorney to create a trust, for example. After that, you will want to monitor the progress your charity is making on its mission and evaluate how effectively it uses gifts from donors. Here again, the three web-based evaluation services mentioned earlier—Guidestar (www.guidestar. org), Givewell (www.givewell.org), and Charity Navigator (www. charitynavigator.org) —can be excellent resources. Annual reports published by the charity can also provide insight into the organization's progress.

COORDINATE YOUR EFFORTS

As with all five areas of advanced planning, charitable giving strategies should not be developed or implemented in a vacuum, separate from your other financial planning initiatives. Coordination is crucial and can be achieved by using a comprehensive approach to wealth management that ensures all decisions reflect your entire financial situation at every step.

In the next chapter, you will see how working with a professional wealth manager will enable you to implement this type of coordinated strategy in the best manner possible.

CHAPTER 14

The Deciding Factor: Getting the Help You Need

You have one more important decision to make. Do you want to handle all the aspects of your wealth management plan by yourself, or would you like to work with someone who can help you design, implement, and monitor your plan?

Many investors, especially those with significant sums to invest, work with professional financial advisors. Should you join them? This chapter will help you with that question—and, if the answer is yes, it will give you tips for finding the right type of advisor to work with.

The fact is, many advisors are not capable of delivering a comprehensive approach like the one outlined in this book, because they simply don't adhere to process we've been exploring. The upshot: If you decide to work with a financial advisor, you need to select one carefully.

SHOULD YOU WORK WITH A FINANCIAL ADVISOR?

These days, it's easier than ever to take a do-it-yourself approach to managing your wealth. Low-cost investments are plentiful. Thanks to the Internet, there are plenty of ways to open an investment account, build a portfolio, and manage it.

So why should you consider getting help? There are some benefits that top financial advisors bring to the table and that are not generally available if you go it alone:

1. Peace of mind. As we've found, many investors are uncertain about the state of their finances. They're not sure how to position their assets. They worry about doing something that could harm their financial health. If they make a change, they second-guess their decisions. Financial advisors help clients by organizing their financial lives, creating customized plans for them, and mapping a way forward. That's a tremendous relief.

2. Discipline. As was explained in chapter 2, emotional responses to the market cause investors to deviate from their disciplined approach—for example, by trying to time the market or chase performance by loading up on investments that have been on a hot streak. Breaking discipline leads to results that can threaten your financial security.

Top financial advisors help ensure that their clients stay on track and don't let emotions break their discipline. One way they do this, as you've seen, is by creating investment policy statements that spell out decision-making criteria. During periods of market stress or euphoria, an IPS can remind investors of their plan and their reasons for investing as they do—and stop them from making rash decisions. Good financial advisors have plenty of experience dealing with market cycles.

They have seen the bad things that can happen when investors break their discipline. They can calm their clients in the face of stressful markets and keep them focused on their goals instead of all the noise.

3. Time. By now, you know what it takes to design, implement, and monitor a successful wealth management plan. From the process of discovery to working on investments, tax planning, wealth transfer issues, asset protection, and charitable giving, a tremendous amount of time is required. What's more, your plan needs to be monitored regularly and refined when major life changes occur. Advisors devote their time to these responsibilities and make sure everything is being taken care of. You need to ask yourself whether you have the time required to do as good a job as a professional can. Even if you think you have the time, ask yourself how you want to spend those hours—coordinating investments and creating complex plans for your assets, or spending time with family and friends and enjoying the life you've worked so hard to build.

4. Expertise. Because of their extensive training, education, and ongoing learning, top wealth managers have a level of expertise and insight that most individual investors don't. That doesn't mean it's impossible for individual investors to succeed on their own. However, the best advisors spend years understanding how the markets work and building investment plans. Most individuals, even the most sophisticated out there, don't have a similar level of training—nor do they have the time or interest in acquiring it.

5. Connections. Even the most capable financial advisors will typically collaborate with experts outside of their firms when a specialist is called for. By working with someone who has deep expertise and who also has a team of experts to reach out to, investors can feel a high level of trust that all facets of their financial lives are being taken care of.

After considering these benefits, do you feel strongly that you have

- the training and experience to make intelligent decisions about your entire financial picture with clarity and certainty?
- the time to build and maintain a comprehensive wealth management plan?
- the discipline to stay on track and rein in your emotional responses?

If so, you may very well be in a position to take full responsibility over your financial life and make all the decisions—large and small—needed to get you to your goals on time with as little stress as possible. However, if you feel you don't have some or all of these qualities, it's worth your time to explore working with a professional.

NINE CRITERIA FOR FINDING THE RIGHT ADVISOR

It's estimated that there are more than 300,000 financial advisors working in the United States. That would suggest that you have more than enough options if you decide to work with an advisor.

Unfortunately, many of these advisors do not offer comprehensive wealth management planning. Some focus on one piece of the wealth management puzzle—investments. Some others focus mainly on pushing products instead of engaging in true long-term, needs-based planning. Those "advisors" are really more like salesmen than true professionals who have your best interests in mind. As you've seen, while it's crucial to get your investments well positioned, it's also vital to address other areas of your financial life.

The scarcity of high-quality advisors is well recognized by

investors. In one study, a mere 2 percent of high-net-worth investors said they planned to recommend their advisors to other people.[16]

All of this means you must be diligent when selecting someone. If you currently work with a financial advisor, you should think carefully about just how satisfied you are with that relationship. Would you refer him or her to a trusted friend or associate? Or are you among the 98 percent of investors who wouldn't?

As you search for an advisor—or re-evaluate your current one—look for one who meets the following nine criteria. The best candidates will stack up well in these categories:

1. The advisor works with you in a fiduciary capacity. Fiduciaries are *legally required* to act in your best interests at all times—they cannot take actions that serve their interests over yours and must provide you with the highest possible standard of care. One way to identify this type of advisor is to ask if they will work with you under the legal standards of a fiduciary and the Investment Advisors Act of 1940.

In stark contrast, other types of financial services professionals must meet a lesser standard of care, called the suitability standard. Advisors who meet the suitability standard are allowed to recommend and sell investments to clients that may not be in their best interests. They may not be required to disclose such information to their clients. For example, they can recommend investments that pay them bonuses or other benefits, even if there are similar investments available that would better match your goals and needs. Such investments might carry much higher expenses than comparable investments.

2. The advisor is fully independent and autonomous. Top advisors will have access to the entire universe of investment products and services. In contrast, some advisors are limited in their choices by the firms they work for. They can only recommend and buy a select group of investments, and those options may not be the best offerings that exist. The same thing applies with outside experts. Independent advisors can choose to work with the best professionals in the business—including top CPAs and attorneys. Other advisors may be limited to their firms' in-house experts, who may not be as well versed in advanced planning issues as other professionals outside of those firms.

3. The advisor is paid through a fee-only compensation agreement. Fee-only means that you will pay the advisor a percentage of your portfolio's assets each year, or an hourly fee. The advisor is not compensated in any other ways. In other words, the advisor's goals are aligned with yours, and there are no conflicts of interest. This structure helps ensure that the advisor gives you the best advice at all times. In contrast, commission-based advisors get paid each time they buy or sell investments in a portfolio. This fee structure may motivate the advisor to make more trades than are necessary, or to select investment solutions for compensation reasons instead of what is in your interest.

4. The advisor focuses on risk tolerance and risk management. Top advisors understand risk management. Taking on more risk than a client can handle comfortably is likely to cause the client to break discipline and deviate from the plan. You should look for an advisor highly focused on helping you figure out your risk tolerance and designing an investment portfolio that meets but never exceeds it. Advisors who advertise their ability to generate huge returns in any or all market environments should be viewed with great skepticism. They are likely to take sizable risks with your assets that could easily backfire and cause you to make rash moves with your money.

5. The advisor is committed to a well-defined investment methodology that you understand and accept. A well-defined investment approach is intended to ensure consistent results over time. The last thing you want is an advisor who uses different investment methodologies from year to year—a sure sign that they are not confident in what they are doing. Ideally, you want advisors to be able to outline a step-by-step process that they use to invest assets and manage wealth overall. What's more, you need to have at least a basic understanding of the advisor's approach and believe in its efficacy. Without this understanding and acceptance, you likely will be tempted to jump ship or demand that the advisor change course whenever the markets are volatile or your portfolio's performance experiences difficulties. It's up to the advisor to be able to explain in plain English what he or she does. If the advisor is unable or unwilling to articulate the approach in detail, be wary.

6. The advisor provides full transparency—in writing—*before* engaging in an advisory relationship. Advisors should be completely up front, open, and clear about the fees they charge and what they deliver for those fees by documenting in writing all fees associated with management of your assets, prior to engaging the relationship. They also should show you, in writing, the specific investments that they plan to use when implementing a wealth management strategy. Finally, they should safeguard their clients' assets with a qualified, third-party custodian. This helps ensure that the assets cannot be stolen or misused by the advisor. In short, you should feel that an advisor has nothing to hide.

7. The advisor is either a Certified Financial Planner or a Chartered Financial Analyst. The CFP and CFA designations are good signs that an advisor has committed to his or her profession and is engaged in ongoing learning, growth, and development as an advisor.

8. The advisor offers consultative wealth management. You can quickly tell whether or not an advisor is consultative. A consultative advisor will spend a great deal of time asking you in-depth questions like the discovery meeting questions detailed in chapter 1. Only then will a consultative advisor begin to develop a plan and make investment recommendations. In contrast, a nonconsultative advisor likely will ask you a handful of basic, cursory questions before suggesting specific investments and products.

9. The advisor is someone you feel you would enjoy working with. Chances are, you will work with your advisor for years (or even decades). So it's important to also pay attention to softer issues like how your personalities match and the overall feeling you get during your interactions. Essentially, you want to have a strong sense that you will work well together, that you will enjoy meeting with the advisor, and that you feel a sense of confidence that the advisor will work hard for you.

ADVISOR INTERVIEW GUIDE

Here are some important questions you should ask advisors when you meet with them. Write down their answers and compare those answers to the characteristics outlined above.

1. Are you held to a fiduciary standard or a suitability standard? Are you legally required to act in my best interests, at all times, with all my funds and various accounts?

2. What professional titles and designations do you hold? What experience do you have as a financial advisor?

3. Are you a Registered Investment Advisor?

4. What services do you offer? How are you set up to help me manage the full range of my concerns?

5. What is your process for working with clients, from the first meeting onward?

6. What is your investment philosophy? What specific criteria do you use to evaluate investment options?

7. Do you have open access to the universe of investment options, or are you constrained in any way?

8. What are your fees, exactly, for each service you provide and overall?

9. How are you paid for your services? Are you compensated for selling one type of investment over another?

10. What steps do you take do avoid any conflicts of interest in your dealing with clients and with providers you work with?

11. How do you custody client assets in a way that ensures they are safe from theft or misuse?

12. What types of clients do you typically work with?

13. Have you ever been penalized, cited, or disciplined by a regulatory organization such as the SEC for unlawful or unethical actions?

14. Will you commit in writing to all recommendations and suggestions for managing my wealth? Will you sign off on this document?

THE JOURNEY AHEAD

At the start of this book, I pointed out that you have a weighty responsibility to make wise decisions about your finances. You owe it to yourself, the people you care about most, and the world around you to be a good steward of all the resources you possess. Your wealth can help you accomplish truly meaningful things in your life—if you manage it well.

Ultimately, wealth management is a liberating experience that relieves you of most—if not all—of the uncertainties we encounter when trying to make smart financial decisions in these complex and challenging times. My clients tell me they feel extraordinarily secure in their ability to live the lives they have planned for, knowing that all the important details are taken care of and that they are positioned to deal with whatever situations come their way. That's a level of comfort—peace of mind—that you may never have experienced before.

So the time has come to ask yourself how you would like to preserve and enjoy your wealth, going forward. You can continue to manage your financial life as you have been, or you can put a sound wealth management process in place and add it to your list of the most beneficial decisions you have made for yourself. I can tell you with the utmost confidence, based on my experience serving clients, that by adopting the approach we've been exploring together, you will put yourself in the best possible position to realize all that is most important to you—and live a life filled with meaning, purpose, and a whole lot of fun. Now that you've read this book, I hope you share that confidence.

The choice is yours. I wish you great success on your journey to a lifetime of comfort, security, serenity, and joy.

NOTES

AUTHOR'S ACKNOWLEDGMENTS

This book would not have been possible without the generous support and collaboration of many professional advisors, clients, friends, and family. Thank you for all your advice and encouragement to see this book through to completion.

Thanks to my brother, Tim, for his ideas and suggestions, for reviewing the chapters, and for helping me to stay on course at every turn. To my colleagues in the office: Tigran Unciano, who worked with me to confirm and consolidate data into charts and illustrations for this book, and Shawna Perow, for keeping me on track.

Thanks to Mark Klimek and Jared Kieling, for their editorial suggestions, guidance, and advice. To Rachel Cooper, Ben Benedict, David Barkhousen, and Jim Pavletich, for their technical editing expertise. Also, Ron VanRell for his research support. To Julie Sendelbach, for helping me successfully navigate past various road-blocks on my way to publishing this book.

Last, I would like to thank my wife, Janelle, and my two kids, Julia and Jameson, for bringing such joy to my life. When I approached Janelle about writing this book and explained the time necessary to complete this project, she didn't hesitate to offer her support. From the beginning, she has been by my side and my number one cheerleader. I am grateful for her encouragement each and every day.

ACKNOWLEDGMENTS
OF PERMISSIONS

Grateful acknowledgment is made to the following organizations for permission to adapt and quote from copyrighted and proprietary materials. These credits constitute a continuation of this book's copyright page.

In the Introduction, under Wealth Management Defined, the wealth management Shorthand Formula and The Consultative Process; in chapter 1, the seven steps of the Discovery Process and the list of Discovery Process Questions; and in chapter 2, the Investment Decision Matrix chart, with accompanying description, and The Emotional Curve of Investing illustration, all from *The Informed Investor: Five Key Concepts for Financial Success* © 2015, 2007 by CEG Worldwide, LLC and from *Cultivating the Affluent*, © 2006 by CEG Worldwide, LLC. All rights reserved. Used by permission.

In chapter 2, statistics on twenty-year historical gains in "Beliefs and behaviors: The key drivers of investors' underperformance" are from page 5 of the 2014 Dalbar, Inc. study, *Quantitative Analysis of Investor Behavior*, © 2014 by Dalbar, Inc. All rights reserved. Used by permission.

In chapter 2, the illustration Reacting Can Hurt Performance and the statistics and charts in the Equities section under "Understand Risk and Portfolio Structure" are adapted for illustration purposes only from "2014 in Review: Small Cap Underperformance," and Long

Term Government Bond data for 1928–2013 is from the *Dimensional 2014 Matrix Book*, © 2014 by Dimensional Fund Advisors. All courtesy of Dimensional Fund Advisors LP.

In chapter 2 and chapter 8, fi360's Fiduciary Score methodology, © 2000–2015 fi360, Inc. Courtesy of fi360, Inc. (www.fi360.com).

In chapter 10, Benefits of Estate Planning, the eight-point list is adapted from the Vanguard investor education brochure *Learn about Estate Planning*.

In chapter 13, in the section A Process for Philanthropic Success, giving preferences and giving options were adapted from content at https://www.vanguardcharitable.org/individuals/resource_center/giving_options/. Items in steps 4-5 and the illustration Charitable Giving Options and related commentary ©Vanguard Charitable 2013. All rights reserved. Used by permission.

ABOUT THE AUTHOR

Jim Hatton, CFP˚, AIF˚ is vice president of Hatton Consulting in Phoenix, Arizona. He and his partners are currently helping more than two hundred families and individuals nationwide manage their personal wealth and guiding them through life's most important financial decisions.

Hatton has been advising clients on wealth management issues for more than fifteen years. He is a Certified Financial Planner, Accredited Investment Fiduciary, and a member of the Financial Planning Association. He holds a BS in Business Administration from Western Michigan University.

INDEX

ENDNOTES

1. Source: Jensen, Michael C. "The Performance of Mutual Funds in the Period 1945-1964," *Journal of Finance*, May 1968. Carhart, Mark M., Jennifer N. Carpenter, Anthony W. Lynch, and David K. Musto. "Mutual Fund Survivorship," unpublished manuscript, September 12, 2000. Blake, Christopher R., Edwin J. Elton, and Martin J. Gruber. "The Performance of Bond Mutual Funds," *The Journal of Business*, 1993: 66, 371-403. Elton, Edwin J., Martin J Gruber, Sanjiv Das, and Matt Hlavka. "Efficiency with Costly Information: A Reinterpretation of Evidence from Managed Portfolios," *The Review of Financial Studies*, 1993: 6, 1-22.
2. *Financial Planning Magazine*, August 2013.
3. www.ssa.gov
4. www.ssa.gov
5. http://www.affordableinsuranceprotection.com/death_vs_disability
6. Inquiry by Kemper, Komisar, and Alecxih taken from Insurance Information Institute. http://www.iii.org/article/will-i-need-long-term-care (Long-term care defined as having limitations on one or more activities of daily living.)
7. Inquiry by Kemper, Komisar, and Alecxih taken from Insurance Information Institute. http://www.iii.org/article/

will-i-need-long-term-care (Long-term care defined as having limitations on one or more activities of daily living.)

8. www.commongood.org/blog/entry/
   infographic-lawsuits-in-america
9. http://www.statisticbrain.com/civil-lawsuit-statistics/
10. www.commongood.org/blog/entry/
    infographic-lawsuits-in-america
11. Patrick L. Remington, Department of Population Sciences, University of Wisconsin School of Medicine and Public Health.
12. www.forbes.com/sites/learnvest/2013/05/16/10-things-you-want-to-know-about-medical-malpractice/ by Demetrius Cheeks.
13. http://www.charitynavigator.org/index.cfm?bay=content. view&cpid=42#.U347yfldV8E
14. http://nccs.urban.org/statistics/quickfacts.cfm
15. Adapted from "Compare giving options." Vanguard Charitable, 2013, https://www.vanguardcharitable.org/individuals/resource_center/giving_options/
16. Tiburon Strategic Advisors, "Financial Advisor Winning Tactics: Defining the Nine Tactical Keys to Success," quoted June 7, 2013, by Warren S. Hersch at http://www.lifehealthpro.com/2013/06/07/high-net-worth-investors-feel-dissatisfied

Made in the USA
Middletown, DE
07 January 2021